SPEAKING OF RELIGIOUS EDUCATION

SPEAKING
OF RELIGIOUS
EDUCATION

GERARD S. SLOYAN

HERDER AND HERDER

1968
HERDER AND HERDER NEW YORK
232 Madison Avenue, New York 10016

Nihil obstat: Donald W. LaRouche, Censor Deputatus
Imprimatur: ✠ Robert F. Joyce, Bishop of Burlington
February 28, 1968

Library of Congress Catalog Card Number: 68–21485
© 1968 by Herder and Herder, Inc.
Manufactured in the United States

CONTENTS

8 6/13

CONTENTS

FOREWORD

IN 1967 I resigned from the faculty of The Catholic University of America, where I had spent seventeen years, and accepted an appointment in the Department of Religion at Temple University in Philadelphia. My chief motivation was the desire to return to fulltime teaching and research. I had never left the classroom, despite the demands of ten years in the department's headship; the work of serious scholarship had suffered badly, however. Two extended entries in an encyclopedia and a half dozen journal articles, the bare minimums for academic promotion, were all I had to show for that decade, when something in another order was being attempted. With one or two exceptions, the essays that follow are selected from several dozens in that line of endeavor, namely popular religious education during the period before and after a major Church council.

When I edited a collection of articles in 1958 entitled *Shaping the Christian Message,* the work of numerous European and a few U.S. scholars, it bore the subtitle *Essays in Religious Education.* This volume was produced under the auspices of the William J. Kerby Foundation to honor its chaplain and my predecessor in academic office, William J. Russell. At the time of its appearance a few of its contributors were already known in this country—Hofinger, Jungmann, Drinkwater, and Weigel —but the greater number like Colomb, Coudreau, Boyer, Delcuve, Ranwez, and Crichton were new names to an American readership. More than that, the term "religious education" was not widely used in the Roman Catholic community. Few were

7

acquainted with the fifty-five-year-old interconfessional associa-
tion and its journal of that title, whereas only a slightly larger
number had heard of an academic department of that name in
Washington associated with educators like Russell and Sheehy,
Cooper, Kirsch and Dowd. It is instructive to read the treatment
of the teaching of religion ("catechetics" was still largely a
seminary word ten years ago) between 1900 and 1950.
Considerable attention was paid to it in National Catholic
Educational Association proceedings, the *Journal of Religious
Instruction* (later *The Christian Educator*), and *The Catholic
School Journal*. The literature was largely given to deploring
the situation, but it did not have many solid proposals to offer.
When Johannes Hofinger of Manila began to appear in the
last-named magazine and in *Worship* in the mid-fifties, even
the most casual reader could tell that this was something new.
The introduction of the notion of the primitive *kérygma* as central, basically the work of Bultmann, Barth, and Dodd though
popularized in German-language Catholic circles by Jungmann
and others, came as a fresh breeze. The entire project of religious
education entered upon a decade of biblical and theological
concern after years of attempted, impossible marriage between
the religion of standard catechisms and the "Munich method"
with its Herbartian steps.

During the decade which the present volume represents, it
seemed important to try to convey to a variety of audiences what
was happening in the Church's public prayer life, its preaching,
and its teaching. This was no recondite knowledge but a body
of theological and pastoral imperatives readily available in
numerous sources. The subject matter was the renewed visage
of the Church, which culminated in the Second Council of the
Vatican. The latter is not to be thought of as initiatory—such
worldwide meetings cannot be, in the nature of the case—but
recapitulatory. Also, in the nature of the case, the life of the
Church has progressed to another point since the 1965 adjourn-

ment of that eventful Council. I do not expect to be in the work of popular education during the period that is upon us, but in the New Testament studies from which I had come. During my tenure as overseer of a department of religious education, however, as president of the Liturgical Conference (1962–64), and as president of the College Theology Society (1966–68), these matters seemed important ones to attend to. One can only wish he had attended to them importantly. Triviality is the curse of journalism and the public lecture. In self-defense, one speaks of the transitory character of all contemporary issues. Actually, this refers to the trivial views a person has held while trying to be profound.

But if the opinions expressed herein are shallow, the causes discussed are deep. They touch on no less than the future of a great communion, the Roman Church, in what is for good or ill the world's most influential nation. A volume of essays provides leaves for the burning, but if Roman Catholic life U.S.A. should be trivial that is another matter. There is some compelling evidence that it is. To point this out cannot be described as taking a popular stance, especially when there are fifty million communicants concerned. It is a much easier matter to speak in praise of vigor, or size, or the one taken for the other. Achievement, however, speaks for itself; it needs no recommendation. Deficiency alone needs loving, careful attention.

By whatever inscrutable design, I was born into a family that was not insecure. There undoubtedly was a "ghetto mentality" in Catholicism but I did not encounter it until I started in at college, where many fellow-students came from the larger eastern cities. My parents were college-educated. I got a reasonably good elementary and secondary schooling, or so it seemed, all under Catholic auspices. Four children in our family went the same educational route, three of them but for the untimely death of one to the Ph.D., sponsored (after college) by a Church that was at least that much interested in higher education. Whether we were affected adversely by the narrowness of our circumstances, or all four proceeded to administer a substandard education under Catholic auspices, is for others to say. My point is that being educated under Church auspices seemed the right thing to do in those years and I have no regrets—only a large measure of gratitude. I have no lifetime to speak of apart from one devoted to Catholic school and adult education. Only the last six months of my life, except for parochial duties on Sunday, constitute a departure from this pattern. The question posed by the essays in this book is not how right what went before was, but how right it is in the present, and will it be in the immediate future?

In today's world large numbers of Catholics are not going to Sunday Mass because it does not "say anything to them." The clergy, when they are alive to the fact of the decline, tend to lose confidence in their ability to "say" what is needed, or else they put it down to the desire for novelty and a general weakening of the faith. Increasing numbers of apostolic workers—clergy and religious chiefly, but not only they—are retiring from their state because they find it an encumbrance or stifling to their personal growth. Fewer and fewer testify that life in the Church, whatever their role in it may be, is an enlarging experience. Much of this may fairly be attributed to the changing times. With or without a Vatican II or a Vietnam there would doubtless have been a black revolution, a sex revolution, a colonial revolution, and a student revolution. Neither Marxism nor Christianity made them. They were simply there: in political consciousness, in literacy and education, in the gospel. The question is, how to deal with them? What is today's answer to the perennial problem of the fitting means of proclaiming in historically conditioned circumstances a gospel that has lasting significance? What cultural forms, what vocabulary, what thought edifices can be used to stand for a God of love whom no man has seen? It is widely being said that neither liturgies nor theologies nor Church structures are of any use in the years that are upon us. Certainly inferior people, or sufficiently endowed people with inferior educations, are not of much use here. Still, one hesitates to say that one cannot think about God (theology), or deal with him imaginatively (liturgy), or seek assistance from fellow-believers (Church structure). What is abundantly clear is that all three need to be improved by way of radical change if they are to attract the notice of that segment of the human race equipped for the prophetic task.

Roman Catholics, like Christians generally, believe that by Christ's promise the Church cannot die. They also believe that they have the power to reduce to impotence the manifestation of that Church, which they are, through neglect. It is to keep this from happening that these essays were written. One hears it said with increasing frequency nowadays, "This diocese is about to explode," "I don't see how that province can last long," "Has religious life any future?", and "One wonders what the Church will look like in twenty years." None of those statements or queries is especially apocalyptic. All are sober observations which could be made by anyone who has eyes to see. One is compelled to set down what one sees, if even a little vision has been given him.

A conservative strain marks most of what is to be found in this book. That is because my chief concern has been to conserve; but only what is worth saving. And I hope I know the difference.

Temple University
Philadelphia, Pa.

GERARD S. SLOYAN

SPEAKING OF RELIGIOUS EDUCATION

1.

Religious Education as a Correlate of "Religious Knowledge": Some Problem Areas*

I should like to approach my subject through an analysis of that catechism most commonly in use in the United States Roman Catholic community, the 1941 revision of the "Baltimore Catechism," so-called, a product of the Third Plenary Council of Baltimore, of 1885. In its spirit it is very much akin to the catechisms of Luther, Calvin, Canisius, Bellarmine, the Westminster, and any you may be familiar with. Basically all can be traced to the Carolingian period, and are derivatives of Augustine of Hippo via Rhabanus Maurus, Honorius of Autun, and Hugh of St. Victor.

Karl Adam in his book *Christ Our Brother* describes our faith in these words:

This is the high mood of Christianity, the holy joy of the redeemed who can no more [i.e., longer] despair for their sins, whose whole life now is centered, not in the struggle with sin, but in love for Christ. Christianity is joy, Christianity is trust, Christianity is constant thanksgiving.[1]

One would not get this impression of Christianity, however, from a reading of *A Catechism of Christian Doctrine, No. 2.*[2]

* First published in *Religious Education*, vol. LXI, no. 4, July-August, 1966, 286–291, 298.

[1] New York, 1962 (1931), p. 49.

[2] Paterson, 1941; a revised edition of the "Baltimore Catechism" of 1885, with a supplement (1961) of 28 questions.

One reason for the revised *Baltimore Catechism*'s failure to present a vivid picture of our faith is its exclusive use of the question and answer method. This method is too weak an instrument to use in the proclamation of the Word which is the Good News, for it makes too objective a thing out of faith. Faith is a reality which must live, but it cannot live if its presentation prescinds from the vital spiritual, economic, or social forces and tendencies of the historical situation in which the believer lives. The exclusive use of the question and answer method means that all children no matter where they live, who they are, or what their backgrounds must memorize not only the same answers but even the same questions; questions which many times have no meaning for them because they would never have thought to ask them, and answers which are often completely divorced from the physically limited but imaginatively rich reality of their lives.

The exclusive use of the question and answer method is a pedagogical strait jacket. To illustrate: the editors of the 1961 supplement to the catechism wished to incorporate the renewed Roman Catholic interest in the Bible—as if the new developments were just a matter of content and not also a new spirit. They were caught, however, by the limits of their method. Since they had not used the Bible in its imagery or its method of presentation in the body of the catechism, they tried to incorporate the "kerygmatic approach" by this question and answer: "What is the chief message of the New Testament? The chief message of the New Testament is the joyful announcement of our salvation through Jesus Christ." Nothing is worse than telling someone that something is joyful when you have not put him in contact with the source of that joy, or with the experience which gives joy its birth. Karl Adam tells us that Christianity is joy, but only after he has placed Christ before our eyes in his works and words of love. Joy is born in no other way.

Even if we prescind from the *Baltimore Catechism*'s exclusive use of the question and answer method, which is in itself a great handicap, what can we say about the quality of the instructional content of this catechism in the light of theological developments at the time of the catechism's revision in 1941?

At least one hundred years before the revision, Johann Adam Möhler had stressed that dogma and doctrine presuppose religious experience, and that the life of the Spirit in us must therefore take priority over the teachings and formulations of faith; Franzelin in the late nineteenth century had said that God speaks not in words alone but also by facts and deeds which are salvation history; John Henry Newman saw revelation not just as a set of propositions but as a historical, mysterious, and religious happening which calls forth a response in man; M. J. Scheeben had rooted theology in Sacred Scripture and in the writings of the Fathers, and had placed Christ our Lord in the center of our supernatural consciousness. For Scheeben the essence of Christianity is primarily not a doing, but a being.

> To be a Christian does not mean, in the first instance, to conform one's way of thinking to God's way of thinking, or to mold one's personality according to the precepts of the New Law. Christianity implies the replenishing and pervading of our spirit with the Holy Ghost, and the engendering of the divine life in our persons.[3]

Emile Mersch, together with Scheeben and Möhler, had stressed the fact that the Church was the mystical body of Christ, each member living the life of the Spirit and united in a living way with Christ, the head of the body. Karl Adam in *Christ Our Brother* (which was translated into English in 1931) had placed Christ in the center of the presentation of faith. In the pages of his book, Christ lives because Adam does not speak of Him in terms of nature and person but in the living language of what Christ has done. In this volume we see Christ's concrete

[3] Cyril Vollert, "Scheeben and the Revival of Theology," *Theological Studies,* 6 (1945), 474.

17

way of teaching, the social sense that love of Christ brings, the banquet and communal aspects of the Eucharist, and sin and repentance, all presented in biblical terms.

The biblical revival in the Roman Catholic Church was well along by 1941, as a glance at the issues of the quarterly journal *Revue Biblique* (Jérusalem, École Biblique) of those years will show. Pope Pius XII's letter on biblical studies in a critical spirit, *Divino Afflante Spiritu,* was just two years away. Yet the spirit which attended both had no influence whatever on the 1941 revision. Rather, the *Baltimore Catechism* of 1941 is still, in the words of Jungmann, a *summula theologica;* it presents the faith to children in language such as: proper object, natural reason, nature and person, evangelical counsels, the distinction between adoration and veneration, between a good reason and a sufficient reason, the conditions for taking an oath licitly, the cardinal virtues, and so forth.

We may say then that neither the theological contributions of Newman, Scheeben, Möhler, Jungmann, or Mersch, nor the results of biblical scholarship of men like Vincent, Lagrange, or Benoit, had any influence whatsoever on the 1941 revision of the *Baltimore Catechism.* A look at Lessons 7 (on the Incarnation), or 11 and 12 (on the Roman Catholic Church and its attributes) or at any of the lessons on the sacraments is clear proof of this.

It may be said in objection that the work of these men—except for that of Adam and Newman—was not available in English until after the revision was made.

An examination of the first fifteen volumes of the periodical *Orate Fratres* shows, however, that the insights of the men mentioned above and what we call new trends in religious education were very much in evidence in the Roman Church in this country in the late twenties and all through the thirties: the Church as mystical body, the sacraments as saving acts of Christ, the Mass as a banquet, the need to learn by doing and not by

18

the memorization of dry formulas, the call for a return to a patristic and biblical type of catechesis, the need to blend catechetics and liturgy, and especially the centrality of Christ in the presentation of the faith—all this and much more was available to the revisers in the pages of *Orate Fratres*. This periodical also included reports of what other nations were doing to revivify the catechetical apostolate.

Therefore both from a pedagogical and a theological point of view, the *Baltimore Catechism* is a painfully inadequate book. The ideal structure of an aid-book for religion study would seem to be one that highlights the love of God who created us and sent his Son to save us, and who sent the Spirit to remain with us in the living Church. Such a volume would bring out the nature of the Christian life as a loving response to the love of God.

One is prone to criticize the heavy use of abstract and notional doctrinal pronouncements, pointing out with Marcel Van Caster that catechesis must aim as much, if not more, at Christian wisdom as at abstract knowledge.[4] Notional pronouncements are not an absolute value in themselves but have a functional role, one of humble service, in bringing a person to open himself to God's summoning Word. Thus the language of the catechism for the most part should be in the prophetic, sapiential, *value-weighted* and experiential language of Scripture itself.

It would seem that for some age groups it is not a question of whether the language of analysis and concepts is better than the symbolic and poetic imagery of the Bible for framing answers to questions. Clearly it is inferior. But one wonders whether the language of "spirit," "breath," "glory," and "power" may not itself be incapable of speaking to the youngest in the catechumenate. The problem posed by the ancient hope regarding catechetical formulas, "they may not understand now but

4 "Wisdom and Doctrine in Catechesis," *Lumen Vitae* 19 (1964) 45–64.

19

they will one day," is just as applicable in this case as in the use of philosophical and creedal language. There are ages when biblical images are understood and appreciated. Without hesitation I can say that the expression of Christian faith in biblical language and its paraphrase can mean much to the adolescent. But in this case the problem takes a special form. It seems to me that the language of the Bible, while it can mean much to the child and adolescent, does not "flex" sufficiently to answer the specific questions he is asking.

Q. Should catechisms ask questions which are answered in biblical language and its paraphrase?

A. There is a time to ask questions and a time to refrain; a time to give answers in the Bible's tongue and a time to talk in the way of Ayn Rand and Mad. For the Spirit speaks to us in Qoheleth, "There is an appropriate time for everything, and a time for every affair under the heavens." (3, 1)

But perhaps it is blameworthy to build on the questionable assumption that there should be such a thing as a catechism in the first place. The criticism suggested by Van Caster might lead to such different kinds of aid-books that we could no longer call them catechisms. In most discussions of catechisms there seems to be the assumption that the book is a fairly complete exposition (the extent of detail depending on the age level) of the truths of faith, whether these be couched in scriptural language or one conditioned by a more recent culture. The assumption which says that catechesis should be built around a book that aims at thoroughness, accuracy, and clarity (at least by way of outline) in presenting the faith, bears examining.

Two areas of thought cause some uneasiness with such an assumption. This brief chapter can only allude to them.

The first cause of uneasiness is the suspicion that the catechism can easily create a harmful illusion. As a neat package of faith, tied up with the ribbon of episcopal approval, the catechism tends to give pastors—and even teachers, with less excuse—the impression that by "teaching" the catechism, they are passing on the faith. Catholics have such a passion for objective, orthodox truth—and for "having" this truth—that they often seem to overlook the fact that for the truth to be truly personal and meaningful to anyone there must be an interplay, a correlation between the recorded truth and the person. It is not enough to be able to read or listen. The individual must experience a need to which a proposed truth corresponds. The truth sets us free—but not just any truth. Libraries are full of truths. Truths can be irrelevant. In Federico Fellini's film, 8½, Guido, besieged by the gnawing emptiness of his life, frantically manages a meeting with the ascetic cardinal in the baths. To his plight, the cardinal responds in the solemn tones of an oracle, "*Extra ecclesiam nulla est salus.*"

Paul Tillich remarks that one of the main difficulties of religious education is that it must give answers to questions that young people have never asked.[5] If they are not brought to ask the questions to which our words about God and Christ, sin and salvation, have the answers, then the truths of faith are like stones thrown at them which sooner or later must fall to the ground. The task of an adequate religious education is to find the existentially important questions which are alive in the minds and hearts of the students. We must make students aware of the questions they already have; then the traditional symbols in myth and cult which were originally conceived as answers to questions implied in man's very existence can be meaningfully passed on. (So Tillich.) But a catechism which has all the answers methodically and logically arranged tends to give answers before questions are asked. All such questions are artificially posed, and overlook the fact that the questions have to be the students' questions.

[5] *Theology of Culture,* New York, 1964, p. 154.

Intellectual doctrine must be taught, but if it is not limited to the measure in which it is seen as a value, the time it took to teach it was wasted. In fact, it may have a positive bad effect, in that when the student reaches a stage where this answer would be of value he fails to seek it out because he has "had that" or "it's kid stuff." Doctrine should not be separated from wisdom, i.e. appreciation of value. The students' stages of development and their experiences and needs will indicate the scope and pace of the instruction as much as—if not more than—the inner logic of the revealed truth itself.

A second source of uneasiness is those recent psychological studies which correlate intellectual training with maturation. From the point of view of the principle of maturation, as Piaget has pointed out, concepts develop in a necessary sequence that is related to age. At each stage of development, the form of a person's thought is determined by factors that are endogenous or internal, while the content of thought is determined by experience. David Elkind of the Child Study Center in Denver applied Piaget's principle to the growth of religious conceptions and the influence of maturation in their development.[6] Children who are exposed to religious teaching eventually come to some understanding of what it means to belong to a particular religion. But Elkind wondered whether this conception of religious identity was entirely due to the effects of religious instruction, or whether its formation was determined, at least partly, by maturation. The results of his study of 800 children, including Catholic, Jewish, and Congregationalist Protestant, over a period of five years, indicated that before the ages of 11 or 12 children are unable to understand religious concepts as they are understood by adults. In fact, they spontaneously give meanings to religious terms that are beyond their comprehension. Though these erroneous ideas are given up spontaneously as the child becomes

[6] "The Child's Conception of his Religious Identity," *Lumen Vitae* 19 (1964) 635–646.

more objective and socialized, the question remains: Is religious instruction worth the effort if the concepts will be meaningless or misinterpreted? Such a question has point if religious education is conceived as a matter of intellect only. True religious education nourishes the emotions as well as the mind. And it is the child's emotions that are ready for religious instruction. A child—surprisingly—is most like adults in his feelings and least like them in his concepts. The child can experience religious emotions before he can entertain religious thoughts. Therefore Elkind concluded that young children should be shown about religion rather than told about it. By taking an active part in liturgy, in customs and celebrations—especially with the family—and by being treated with consideration and respect in these activities, the child builds up an emotional religious life. For children, religion is first of all feelings and action within the sphere of the actions of the Church.

If faith is thought of as essentially a system of formulated dogmas, or if it is thought of almost exhaustively as propositional truth, then it will not only be acceptable but even mandatory to teach Christian doctrine in the way of the catechism. Today, as we look back we see a tendency that might be called religious anthropological "extrinsicism."

Kant did much to destroy, if not this concept of faith, at least the epistemological basis on which it rested. The Protestant apologetic movement dating from this period was an attempt at the transitions necessary to make revelation and man at least compatible. There is some indication that Catholic thinkers were later willing to make the same adjustments, but this attempt could not come to fruition because of the Roman Church's historic struggle with "modernism." Only after many hesitant steps could the Catholic mind comfortably make the necessary distinction between the transcendent human spirit as it confronts the transcendence of God who reveals himself, and the human spirit that creates, fashions, and projects these truths. It

23

took such thinkers as Newman and Blondel to make these distinctions, but it will take even longer for this thought to penetrate the reflective consciousness of Catholic thought and life. Again, until this personalism of Kierkegaard, Newman, and Blondel can enter the bloodstream of the Roman Church's thinkers and find at the same time a natural sympathy in the lived experience of the faithful, until there takes place a shift in man's view of himself along certain lines suggested by Darwin, Marx, and Freud, until man has a new anthropology with which to work, faith can only be conceived of as a strictly and essentially propositional matter.

If, however, we make a shift in emphasis so that the encounter of faith contains a new type of personalism and anthropology, and if this new type finds a certain sympathy in the thought patterns of modern man, then we are faced with two alternatives. Either we continue to think of revelation as the imposition of absolute truth, and faith as man's assent to it, thereby running the risk of extrinsicism, dechristianization, and indifference; or we speak of revelation and faith as the I-thou encounter through the historic, saving events in the life of Christ as now lived in the experience of the Church. In the first alternative, propositional truth and the constant rephrasing of propositional truth will serve the cause in an adequate fashion. In the second, there will be a demand for the retention of propositional truth, but there will also be a clear demand that the reality of salvation continue in the life and witnessing of the Church, in Word and Sacrament as spoken and done by this community.

But even in the second alternative, it will only be a question of old wine in new skins if it is not adequately conveyed that this reality of salvation is the personal communication of the triune God to man in the person of Jesus Christ, and that man must take a position before this personal communication in Christ.

The two concepts of faith are different, but not necessarily

24

opposed. The first sees faith as a supernaturally entitive quality alone; the second feels a need to say something about the conscious counterparts of faith in the light of human psychology.

The recent writing of men such as Tillich, Buber, Jean Mouroux, and Roger Aubert, to name the obvious ones, would seem to indicate that the second alternative is more in keeping with the mentality of the Scriptures. The theological reflections of men such as Barth, Rahner, and Schillebeeckx, again to name only the obvious ones, have clearly indicated the insufficiencies of a theology of faith-revelation which accepts solely and exclusively propositional truth. The recent reflections of the Second Vatican Council on revelation indicate how these insights, once the private possession of a gifted few, are now finding their way into the reflective consciousness of the Church. It will be a natural consequence that the act of faith will be reconsidered.

A doctoral candidate did a thesis under my direction a few years ago which established that in the twelfth through sixteenth centuries the adult catechetical treatises on grace (divine life, trinitarian indwelling) ran at least two hundred years behind theological development. That is the great challenge to the Roman Catholic community now: to see that the solid progress of our biblical and systematic theologians who are men of great faith, and of our few perceptive sociologists and psychologists, makes its way fairly swiftly into the area of religious education, where we haven't a moment to lose.

Historically, the catechism which came from the Third Plenary Council of Baltimore showed the influences of Augustine's method, of Bellarmine's approach, of other unknown historical inspirations. Theologically, it could only be the reflection of the thought that prevailed for many centuries, based as it was on a particular conception of the nature of the act of faith. Grace was considered throughout the catechism mainly in its effects, namely as a quality in man, rather than as a cause, namely, the divine action. Finally, the emphasis in the sacraments was on the

25

effective working of these signs if no obstacle of sin is placed.

It seems clear that a national catechism even for adults would be out of place at the present time. Contemporary theological thought is only in its adolescent stage, and any attempt to give it final expression, even catechetically, will be truncated and incomplete. Moreover, what is expressed nationally frequently carries with it the hallmark of permanence. There is the question, is it possible to write such a catechism in the light of the new insights? Time must suspend a definitive answer on this point; there may come a time when we will feel that there is a real necessity. In the meantime, there will always be a suspicion that such a catechism will, because of the terms of its intent, tend to extrinsicism, even to nominalism. Past history will make us cautious, the thought of Rahner and Tillich will suggest hesitancy, and the fear of infidelity to theological insight would seem to suggest that a national catechism is essentially a hindrance. The recent volume from Holland, *De Nieuwe Katechismus,* probably cannot be duplicated within this century. In any case, it seems needless to try until the circumstances of its sponsorship begin to prevail here.

2.

Teaching a Personal Relation to Father, Son, and Spirit*

The grandmother didn't want to go to Florida. She wanted to visit some of her connections in east Tennessee and she was seizing at every chance to change Bailey's mind. Bailey was the son she lived with, her only boy. He was sitting on the edge of his chair at the table, bent over the orange sports section of the *Journal* . . .

She called out to him that a convict called the Misfit had escaped out of the federal prison in Florida and they might all get "murderized."

Bailey didn't look up from his reading so she wheeled around then and faced the children's mother, a young woman in slacks, whose face was as broad and innocent as a cabbage and was tied around with a green headkerchief that had two points on the top like a rabbit's ears. She was sitting on the sofa, feeding the baby his apricots out of a jar. "The children have been to Florida before," the old lady said. "You all ought to take them somewhere else for a change so they would see different parts of the world and be broad. They never have been to east Tennessee."

The children's mother didn't seem to hear her but the eight-year-old boy, John Wesley, a stocky child with glasses, said, "If you don't want to go to Florida, why dontcha stay at home?" He and the little girl, June Star, were reading the funny papers on the floor.

"She wouldn't stay at home to be queen for a day," June Star said without raising her yellow head.

* Based on an article first published in The Living Light, vol. 2, no. 2, Summer, 1965, 22–34.

"Yes and what would you do if this fellow, the Misfit, caught you?" the grandmother asked.

"I'd smack his face," John Wesley said.

"She wouldn't stay at home for a million bucks," June Star said, "Afraid she'd miss something. She has to go everywhere we go."

"All right, Miss," the grandmother said. "Just remember that the next time you want me to curl your hair."

June Star said her hair was naturally curly. . . .

[The next day].

"Let's go through Georgia fast so we won't have to look at it much," John Wesley said.

"If I were a little boy," said the grandmother, "I wouldn't talk about my native state that way. Tennessee has the mountains and Georgia has the hills."

"Tennessee is just a hillbilly dumping ground," John Wesley said, "and Georgia is a lousy state too."

"You said it," June Star said.[1]

June Star, John Wesley, and the Grandmother all proceeded to other concerns before the day was over, but that is not my point for the moment. My point is that these three people are our culture. They are our people; they are ourselves, God's people. In ten or twelve years the children will be making application to the college of their choice.

The Church's vocation as bride of the Lamb (Apoc. 21, 9) —as city built foursquare—is to invite them into that city where the lamp is the Lamb, where the glory of God gives light, and there will be no night.

Meanwhile, in the *kaíros* or season that is every man's time of pilgrimage, "Tennessee is just a hillbilly dumping ground, and Georgia is a lousy state too." You said it.

Our questions here should be two: what is the Church up to, and what does she think she is up to, as she goes on pilgrimage over the ages? This must first be known before it can be com-

[1] From "A Good Man Is Hard to Find," in *3 by Flannery O'Connor*, New York, 1964, pp. 129–31.

municated. It must be realized as something worth communicating.

The Church is the savior of men. Of course God alone is man's savior, his liberator or redeemer in any ultimate sense. He does the work of restoration, of removing burdens from our backs and enlarging to full human stature through the Church. But the Church is his Son in our flesh, written large in the cosmos—"the universe, all in heaven and on earth . . . brought into a unity in Christ . . . [when the time was ripe]." (Eph. 1, 10)

The design of God, His will or counsel as the New Testament calls it, is to achieve in us men a slow integration whereby we are whole once again or whole in quite a new way. The agency He chooses to achieve this is the body and spirit of Christ which will act effectively on our body and spirit. Jesus Christ, in whom in His present state of glory man is perfectly reconciled to God (see 2 Cor. 5, 18f.), is not simply the image or archetype of what we are meant to be, what we are called to be. He is in his own person the instrument of our salvation. The more especially in His manhood, the more particularly as He is man, is He the instrument of our integration, which is none other than our salvation.

We have been told how this is to come about.

In faith we know that the gospel is to be preached to men (see Rom. 10, 8–17). The message of how they shall be whole again must be proclaimed in their hearing. But of course tidings and person, message and man, are one: the Lord Jesus, in whose dying our death is destroyed and by whose rising our life is restored (see the Easter Preface of the Roman Missal).

Now that means that Jesus must come alive in human life—in human lives:

—Jesus, the compassionate, the fellow-sufferer;

—Jesus, to whom life is a scandal, as it is to every one of us; to whom human existence is anguish;

—Jesus, the Victor, whose conquest of death is the basis of our hope (cf. 1 Cor. 15, 25f.). A hardship for the Christian adult is that Jesus is presented as so victorious from the moment of His conception that He really cannot be known to suffer—or can be thought of as suffering only in the sense of enduring pain, understood as something that hurts—and since that isn't the sense in which most men endure pain throughout most of their lives, He is no sign of hope to them;

—Jesus, the man of free and independent choice, whose openness to the absolute word of God led him fearlessly to wherever the will of God expressed in that word took him;

—Jesus, the non-conformist, the despiser of hypocrisy in whatever form it happened to be enshrined, whether sacred or secular, civil or religious; the one to whom hypocrisy or inauthenticity was anathema—who would not fall in line with anything that smacked of hypocrisy;

—Jesus, the reliever of the oppressed, the man who "feels" for other men and acts on His convictions, which are not alien to His feelings.

Now it is He, this Jesus, who is the way to the Father. A Counselor or Advocate other than Himself is the one who will lead us to the Father. (Cf. Jn. 14, 16. 26; 15, 26.) So much does He want us to be men of faith and not sight that He insists it is necessary that He go (cf. Jn. 16, 7) if the Spirit is to accomplish His work—which of course is the Father's work—in us.

The entire emphasis of Holy Scripture and the Church Fathers is on the personal *Spirit* whom God sent to men; on *Christ* who abides in us through the Spirit's agency or action; on *God* who shows mercy by communicating himself to justified men through this Spirit. In other words, He whom theology calls the "un-created Gift" of God—God, self-given to mankind—is primary in human holiness. Every created grace, every alteration of our human characters and personalities, every way of man's being made more in God's image (*pneumatikós* or "spirit-ed," as the Fathers would say) is a consequence and a manifestation of this uncreated grace who is God, self-given to men through the Son, in the Spirit.

The word trinity is the result of the stress on the divine unity. This stress had currency in the West chiefly, though the Greek-speakers adopted a word for use just as the Latins did (*triás* being a noun in ordinary usage to describe three of anything). In either language the term was a response by those Christians who feared that the oneness of God, his *monarchía* or unity, whether taken with respect to the divine essence or in a context of origination within the godhead, was threatened. They thought it threatened by the Christians who spoke too constantly and too freely of deity as "three," in the manner of Holy Scripture and the writers of the first two centuries. The threateners were those who were at ease in face of the notion of the deity as a distinct three, or the idea of three in the deity who were distinct. The response to this conception was a term ("trinity") which stood for the reality of the unity of the divine being, the "monarchy" or godhead.

Augustine made an important contribution in his concern for "substantial relations"; this idea Thomas Aquinas took up and developed. The history of the doctrine of the divine Trinity tells us how, after Augustine in the West, the mystery of the triune God became for Christians the mystery of God as He is in himself. This development was the result of Augustine's thought. Our trinitarian theology, preaching, and catechetics became a consideration of God's inner nature apart from any special relation of this mystery to us, other than that the summit of Christian faith was to believe in it.

Priests do not preach on the Trinity very often, one supposes, not because they do not comprehend the catechesis they are given in seminaries on this mystery but for two quite different reasons: that they cannot express this mystery in ordinary language, and that it does not mean anything important to them in their own lives. They do not feel a strong, inner compulsion to speak of God as He is in himself, in the way in which the non-biblical language of theology elaborates this mystery.

In the apostolic age God was known as three in terms of His action in human life. The uniqueness of this revelation can be understood adequately only in a context of the whole story of salvation. First, God was active, speaking to His people over the ages and requiring a free and responsible answer on their parts. This divine action was the working out of a plan or purpose which came to its fullness in Christ. (Cf. Eph. 1, 3–14.) The revelation of the plan in Christ is the climax of God's self-revealing activity; it is, in some sense, His last act on the human scene. (Cf. Eph. 1, 22f.; 3, 11; 4, 13.) He means to do no more, no better, no further in our behalf. Never again will this design of His to save us be surpassed. This final act of revelation is, at the same time, the final act of salvation. In other words, we can know something of how He is Father, Son, and Spirit only if we know what he does in the person of Jesus Christ. (Cf. Rom. 8, 14–17.)

When the first letter of John says that God is love (4, 16), this means two things: that God in His inner life is love, and that God in His dealings with man is love. He is love in Himself, a union and giving among three Persons. But that is a matter unknown to us, and we may even say freely, unknowable to us, without the knowledge of the self-donation of the three to us in Jesus Christ.

In the first chapter of St. Paul's letter to the Ephesians quoted above at verse 10, which contains the well-known phrase about "bringing all into unity in Christ," these other phrases flank that much-quoted verse: "Praise be to the God and Father of our Lord Jesus Christ, who has bestowed on us in Christ every spiritual blessing in the heavenly realms. In Christ he chose us before the world was founded . . . to be accepted as his sons through Jesus Christ, that the glory of his gracious gift, so graciously bestowed on us in his Beloved, might redound to his praise."

We have two persons and an action: *theós* and *iēsoûs christós* and a *prógnōsis* or *boulē'*, a design, a will in our respect. How will it end? "That the glory of his gracious gift will redound to his praise"—in other words, glory coming out from God, going, through Christ, back to God. "He has made known to us his hidden purpose . . . that the universe, all in heaven and on earth, might be brought into a unity in Christ." (v. 10) And Paul goes on: ". . . When you had heard the message of truth, the good news of your salvation, and believed it, you became incorporate in Christ and received the seal of the promised Holy Spirit; and that Spirit is the pledge (the *arrabō'n*, or "down-payment," as we would say) that we shall enter upon our heritage, when God has redeemed what is his own, to his praise and glory." (vv. 13f.)

Now in that passage—and it is typical of New Testament trinitarian teaching—we see the role of each of the three brought out clearly. There is initiation out of love by the Father; there is the mediatory role of Christ; and there is the sanctifying action of the Spirit, who is given as the sign of all that is to come when we are brought into cosmic unity in Jesus Christ. The work to be accomplished intermediately is that we should be sons in Christ; but in the end, God's praise or glory—which is very much a thing He himself accomplishes in us—is what must be achieved. God is not seen as receiving this praise and glory except through the achievement of sonship in us.

The point is that we learn of the interior trinitarian relations of the godhead from the apostolic teachers only incidentally to the sphere of grace, uncreated Grace. We learn principally of those three who are self-given. Created grace, the difference in us once we have received them or let them come to us, is a secondary concern of the New Testament. It is described chiefly in terms of our sonship of God.

As the crises of the Arian heresy (denial of the Son's divinity) and the Macedonian heresy (denial of the Holy Spirit's divinity) arose, there flourished the tendency known as "economic trinitarianism." This notion, which later came to be considered heresy, holds that God is not three in essence but only three in His operation in the creation and salvation of men. We can see immediately why it is heretical, and why it contains the material for a great heresy: it is so largely true. God does not become Father, Son, and Spirit in saving men, but it is only in His saving them that we know He is Father, Son, and Spirit.

The knowledge we have of the divine Trinity from the New Testament is above all personal. We are introduced to three (although often two at a time, so that there is every ground for a binitarian heresy in the New Testament: a Father-Son pair, who have a little brother like Miss O'Connor's John Wesley, the Holy Spirit). In any case, there are three who are distinct for the apostolic teachers, and whose happiness we are invited to share. We are told that our fulfillment and God's glory, together, consist in our going back to *theós* (God), and that it is the *pneûma* (Spirit) who will see to this. He will see to it in this life. He will make us sons as a kind of prognosis or indication of what this sonship may come to be once it is brought to perfection.

You do not find in the New Testament any of the remoteness in conceiving God that tends to separate most Christians from the Father, Son, and Spirit. We even speak nowadays of "the forgotten God" who is the Holy Spirit. That is a kind of sick joke: that the Holy Spirit could ever be referred to in Christian circles as forgotten. We concede that Christianity has been evacuated of its meaning when we make such an admission about the place of the Holy Spirit in our lives. The first Christians did not know God so much as one—Father, Son, and

Spirit—who had acted to save them, as God who had acted to save them through His Son in the Holy Spirit. The difference in stress is very important. If we continue to teach God as He is in Himself, the inner trinitarian relations in other words, we are fated to make Him meaningless. If we say that "the Trinity" acted to save us, such a statement is simply unfaithful to the New Testament deliverance as it comes to us.

The catechetical problem, it would seem, is how these words or ideograms "God," "Son," and "Spirit" stand for the three greatest realities in human life, which are one reality.

One keeps thinking of people the age of John Wesley and June Star. They are eight and ten at the moment, and they are driving to Florida. Will those three words ever stand for the reality of love that enters into their lives, or will they merely live out their lives and get Christian burial?

All of us know some genuinely committed Christians who have been made such by God's action in the Church. But we need to worry about the obstacles we have set in the way, or what is wrong with our work that it doesn't happen often enough. We are right in assuming there is no flaw in the work of the Holy Spirit. Why do we not let him form Christians in the image of God's Son more often?

The catechist knows that he has the problem of analogy. He knows that God can only be taken in by men by way of symbol. We men cannot know Him as the infinite, the absolute; we would have to be the infinite and the absolute to know Him as He is. So we use the symbols with which He has provided us, such as our faith and the language of faith. They stand for God with sufficient accuracy that we may really believe in Him and not in the symbols.

Paul Tillich's solution is a radical one. He says we can know something of the ground of our being, that which underlies our existence, the absolute, only through giving answer to its unconditional demands. Who is God? He is the one who underlies all my life, the lives of all men within the compass of that universe which is other than He. He is the one who sustains and supports us, and we come to know Him through giving answer to His unconditional demands.

Rudolf Bultmann would say that Jesus is the one who put the fewest conditions on His response. He was authentically Himself because he took seriously and without reservation all the moral and political choices He was faced with, most especially the challenge of the cross. Tillich would say of Jesus that He looked within to the creative ground and meaning of our existence and was ultimately concerned over it. Dietrich Bonhoeffer speaks of God as "the beyond in midst of our life." Søren Kierkegaard refers to a "deeper immersion in existence."

Is this line of thought "immanentism"? Do we simply dismiss it by tacking a label on it? There is, in fact, nowhere to go except to the depths of one's own consciousness to know God. We cannot flee to any other place—if you will excuse the spatial metaphor in a Bultmannian context. We can only know Him by looking within (assuming the necessity of first taking in the world through the senses). In the depths of our being we discover Him through use of the right symbols such as "Father" and "Son." "Philip, he who has seen me has seen the Father." These ideograms are taken out of human reality. There are fathers and sons only in human families. The words are sufficiently helpful to give us some clue to the divine reality. We come to this reality only in the depths of our consciousness.

Is God personal? We Christians have always answered "Yes" to that. We have been saying lately, with intensity of conviction, "He is above all personal," and, "The Christian does not 'know' God unless he is in an intimate, personal relation with him." God is personal, Tillich would say, in the sense that ultimate reality underlies all that we experience as personal. "God is love" (John's phrase) means that in pure personal relationship we encounter the deepest truth about reality. God is the one who gives Himself most fully without hope of return. This being so, only the man who has loved can say what God is.

One definition of God, we have indicated, might be "the self-given"—by which is meant, in first place, the interiorly self-given as among Father, Son, and Spirit. But in this sense, it may reasonably be asked, "Who cares?" We care, because God is the self-given to us as well. If you have loved you can know Him whose definition is that He is love. If you have not loved you can never know this by being told that He is love. What is specifically Christian about our view of the world is that we assert that *the final definition of the reality of personal relationship is the love of God in Christ Jesus our Lord.*

Now, how is all this our problem? The catechist is someone who must know the great realities of life. God must be real to him. However, God's personality is, as Rudolf Otto suggests, the visible, conceptualizable "one-tenth of an iceberg" that shows. The rest, the other nine-tenths, is the numinous that we take in non-rationally.

I do not wish merely to parrot the ideas of deep thinkers. I do wish to say that I think that many of these ideas are right. If we teach God as a person (I mean God the Father) as if we could understand Him fully in his personality, the eight-year-old child will know that we are wrong. He senses immediately that God is much more mysterious than that, at which point the catechist has lost the eight-year-old child. God our Father is chiefly incomprehensible mystery to us, with a little bit of what we call "personality" showing. Christ is the sacrament of God. He is one in whose presence His fellows felt inadequate: dust and ashes. "Go, Lord, leave me, sinful man that I am," said Peter (Luke 5:8). Christ is definable personality, as we know it, in a way that His Father is not—though during his lifetime His Father *was* such a definitive personality to Him. We do not suppose for a moment, however, that the Father of Jesus Christ can be Father to us in exactly the same way He was Father to

Him. The Spirit is that breath or force or power that makes men love, that is responsible for superhuman realities in the midst of men. Do men do a thing that is beyond their powers? It is the Spirit who is responsible for it. He is person from the very fact that his divine power underlies all that persons do that is quite beyond themselves.

The catechist, in knowing those three great realities, Father, Son, and Spirit as they can be known, will necessarily know them through the signs which stand for them best. He must know those experiences that evoke the reality of God's action in men's midst most effectively. Which are the experiences that evoke the reality of God's action best? They are chiefly sacramental experiences steeped in charity, and after that, all other experiences of love than the sacramental ones. I mean to designate as the best signs of the three persons in God, human interpersonal love-relations: experiences had both with the aid of sacramental signs and apart from sacramental signs.

We have said that the catechist must know those words which interpret best the meaning of God's action in the midst of men. Now those words are chiefly but not exclusively the words of Scripture. Often biblical speech is conceptual, but sometimes it is not. This is not to say that the testimony to God's word comprised by the Bible has no idea-content. Obviously it does. I am thinking, for the moment, of the Isaian Apocalypse (chapters 24–27), or a little snatch out of the Book of Revelation such as 21, 1–7, or the entire fourth gospel, where the reality of God's action is interpreted to us verbally, but non-rationally as much as rationally. Speaking in tongues, as it was incoherently done in the early Church and occasionally today, is a possible manifestation of God's action.

The catechist must use interpersonal relations for what they are. They are the clearest sign and best analogy for the saving work of God among men. At times we unquestionably feel that we must write off words such as "lambs," "shepherds," and

38

"good seed." "Father" is of no help at all in situations where young people despise that word because of the reality it stands for in their lives. The same is true of "son" for the girl of nine who should have been a boy; by now the notion of sonship is hateful in her ears. We do, therefore, write off certain words as being of little help in conveying the great realities, knowing that we have to find better ones to convey what they stand for. The first reality in every situation is the relation of love among persons. That is what is signified, whether by the sheep-shepherd image which says love to some, or the father-son image which says it to others. What is the reality behind all these symbols? It is the charity that enlarges, the charity that frees, the charity that is solicitous, the charity that heals.

For the Christian there is no such thing as "mere humanism." By definition we are a people who cannot be "too humanistic." We consult the needs of each other's manhood, and in so doing we discover God. The loves with which we love are divine loves. We have been told that in faith. We must expand them and explore them so as to live eternally by them.

What, in fact, do we do? We choose signs that smother, signs that lead away from the God within. Even when we have the right signs, such as the sacraments, we tend to do the wrong things with them.

There is another story in 3 by Flannery O'Connor called "A Temple of the Holy Ghost." In it a girl of twelve is involved in a home visit with two girls of fourteen; the two older ones go to a circus, a country circus in the south, and at a sideshow they see a hermaphrodite. Later the little girl wants to know what they saw. She bargains with them: "I saw rabbits born once and I'll tell you how they are born if you tell you what you saw at the sideshow." Then they explain how the freak, as he is called, walks on either side of a curtain, lifting his dress to the people on each side and saying in a mournful tone, "I'm going to show you this and if you laugh, may God strike you the same way. . . . This is the way He wanted me to be and I ain't disputing His way. . . . I'm making the best of it. I don't dispute hit."

The little girl has learned from the two week-end visitors that in their convent school they have been described by a Sister who teaches them as "temples of the Holy Ghost." The Sister says they should tell boys who get fresh in the back seats of cars, "I am a temple of the Holy Ghost." The little girl who has been told the story of the freak, in keeping her part of the bargain, says that the mother rabbit spit the baby rabbits out of its mouth. That night, lying in bed, she tries to work the whole thing out. How can a freak like that be a temple of the Holy Ghost? What the child has done is discovered a real life problem. It is right for her to have it. She also has a fitting sign, the person's strange body and tortured mind. God's love is unquestionably manifest somehow in this poor creature, who is making his (her?) living this way.

At the end of the story, they go back to the convent school where the two are deposited on a Sunday afternoon. In three minutes at the very close, the child is smothered in various signs of Christian faith. As soon as they come to the door they are bundled off by a Sister who meets them at the door to the chapel, where benediction is in progress. I need not tell you what the smothering signs are. Well-worn hymn tunes, the air heavy with incense, the monstrance held aloft, the host shining out ivory-colored in the center.

The mystery of the eucharistic body of Christ is totally concerned with the way in which the Spirit-filled, risen Jesus makes us temples of the Holy Ghost. The sign has never said anything remotely like that to the child. One has the feeling it never will. And all during Benediction, the little girl is thinking of the tent at the fair with the freak in it. The freak was saying, "I don't dispute hit. This is the way He wanted me to be."

Putting the case of the relation of sign to ultimate reality another way, we might refer to the film *Becket.* There is a scene in it in which the King of England is discovered by his friend Becket in a compromised position with a young woman. The king is defensive but by no means embarrassed. Becket at this point in the film is already showing signs of religiousness. The king pats the rump of his little friend through her filmy night-dress and says to him, "Round and firm as an apple! You have your world, Becket; I'll have mine."

Now in some way this is the catechist's problem. Half the world has a cosmos under its palm: an immediate, easy-to-interpret sign of ultimate reality, whatever that reality may be. At first the sign is thought to stand for pleasure without pain: the pleasure of a human relationship without responsibility. The sign stands immediately for the urge to creativeness, the urge to be fruitful. But, more basically, the world under the palm is a sign of an interpersonal relation, for the man is accepted by another, and he accepts her. Even though we say that the terms of the relation are bad, it is its power as an anodyne that recommends it. A man can endure a lot in virtue of those intervals in which Eve is seen as herself the paradise of pleasure.

The chief problem of religious formation is that of helping men to regulate their love lives. They need to put *éros* in the service of *agápē* or, if that figure of submission is bad, relate *éros* and *agápē* as they must be related. In a word, religious formation consists in providing an experience of human love which will at the same time be divine love. This will be the case necessarily if it is experienced by Christians in the way they ought to love. It will be human love transcended, transformed.

The right signs will be made to stand for the right realities, the ultimate ones, in the minds of those who are taught. And in that establishment of a correct relation between reality and sign, good religious education consists.

3

Examining the Language of Faith*

The other evening I met Father Avery Dulles from Wood-
stock College on a plane bound for Chicago from the Baltimore
airport, and I said to him at the end of the trip: "You don't
normally expect to see Dulles flying out of Friendship." He said
he was going to the Second International Ecumenical Congress
at Western Michigan University, and was holding in his hand a
book called *The Secular Meaning of the Gospel* by a student of
Karl Barth named Paul Van Buren who teaches at Temple
University in Philadelphia. He confided he thought it might
be hard for him to be fully ecumenical in spirit for the next
four days because he disagreed with every second sentence in the
book. I assume that the meeting went well enough. I have here a
story from the *National Catholic Reporter* of August 18, 1965
on what happened at it, and should like to share with you some
of the thoughts of Dr. Van Buren. He will do admirably, I think,
as a representative of a stream of thought it is important for
us to be acquainted with and in some measure to be in.

Van Buren is quoted as having asserted, "Perhaps the Good
News is not that there is a God but that there is a neighbor
and this, when truly heard, can be a word as rich in mystery,
wonder, and power, as any man has spoken about God." The
Reporter goes on to say that the thread that ran through the
congress was that for good or ill the secular age is upon us and

* Address delivered at the Northeast Seminarian Study Conference meeting, August 26, 1965.

man has taken over his own destiny. Harvey Cox's *The Secular City* makes the same point, more or less, though Cox is insistent that modern man has a better chance to be free under God, in the biblical sense, than ever before. Another essay you are undoubtedly acquainted with is in Bishop J. A. T. Robinson's chapter "Worldly Holiness" in *Honest to God* on the essentially sacred nature of one's call in the secular order.

The strongest statement of the problem under discussion came in the Western Michigan talk when Van Buren disputed traditional ways of talking about God and religion. He said, "Neither God nor belief in him has much to do with the best of today's behavior. Divine power and joined forces, the realm of the supernatural, no longer count as important or even real factors in our understanding of the way things are and how they work." "Such terms as forgiveness, love, justice, mercy, freedom, may have grown out of Christianity," he added, "but younger theologians now recognize that these terms have been absorbed and practiced by persons and social movements quite apart from and sometimes in conscious rejection of Christianity." "You might say that forgiveness, honor, love, justice are part of the recognizable vocabulary of Christian faith." Van Buren went on to describe today's world as "the breaking point between an old and a new culture." Men think in entirely different terms and concepts. Old words and concepts do not carry their meaning across cultures. "We must realize that when we use the term 'God' we are talking about something which no longer connects with anything in most people's minds except whatever happens to be left over after all the vital connections are made."

A comment was made to a reporter during the congress by a theology teacher of the Episcopal diocesan seminary in Michigan to the effect that Dr. Van Buren is difficult to assess because he is so philosophically-minded that everything is tentative. The observer added, however, that one of the things Van Buren is saying is that "if the Church is going to communicate with people, it must start listening to what the world is saying, and what the world is saying is good."

Writing in the journal *Religious Education* under the title "Post Mortem Dei" Van Buren makes the point—one which has been made a number of times by Professor John McDermott of Queens College, New York, most recently in the Winter, 1965 *Cross Currents* ("The American Angle of Vision" [XV, 1, 69–93])—that modern Western man, specifically men of this continent, do not have as their metaphysic the metaphysic of biblical theology or of Thomism or of Heidegger. What they have is a rough-hewn, man-in-the-street, general, technological, Western approach to life, says Van Buren, somewhat empirical, somewhat pragmatic, somewhat relativistic, somewhat naturalistic, but also somewhat aesthetic and personalistic. He goes on to say that the virtue of this commonsense metaphysic or whatever you wish to call it is that most men to whom you are trying to preach the gospel possess it. They live by it even unconsciously. It is their thought-structure, insofar as they have one. If any values whatever are to be proposed to them they must be proposed in terms of this metaphysic; the only claim we can make with hope of success, says the Temple professor, is an appeal to its descriptive character. We are forced to say that this metaphysic is more widely shared than are the metaphysical assumptions in terms of which the gospel is normally presented. For purposes of doing theology today (and I might add catechetics), Van Buren proposes that we explore the possibilities of working on this common ground. Another idea he puts forward is that one feature of contemporary secular culture is its almost exclusive concern with contemporaneity. The past is not of great moment to most of us most of the time.

I take this last idea to be an axiom. Modern catechetics is going on the error of assuming that the sacred past is of considerable concern to the parishioner in the pew and the pupil in the classroom. It is a false assumption, yet we go on it all the time.

The past is of no avail, says Van Buren, unless it becomes somehow contemporaneous for the believer. That, I suggest, should be a Christian axiom; it is the substratum of our celebration of the mystery of Christ in the liturgy and the underpinning of any realistic catechetics.

Marx and Freud have played their part in defining the man Jesus as the man for others; not that Marx was interested in Jesus as the man for others. The development of the Western understanding of man in the nineteenth century separates a Bonhoeffer and a Robinson from a Luther or a Calvin. If you read Luther or Calvin you discover that they are going on the same set of assumptions as the language of a textbook in Catholic theology written twenty years ago. (For a good theoretical discussion of this question, namely, why the nineteenth century does not speak to the sixteenth, or, for that matter, to the eighteenth, you might be interested in an essay by Johannes Metz in Volume 6 of "Concilium," *The Church and the World*, entitled "Unbelief as a Modern Problem.") Van Buren says that the work of the Christian educator is to serve faith by teaching an old, old story; by making it familiar; by tracing different ways in which it has been, and can be, told. The Christian educator does not *preach*, in other words suggest the relation of the story to the hearer's life. That is for lectern and holy table. He *teaches* the story as story, however.

Van Buren is making a distinction here between the didactic function of the liturgy and extra-sacramental catechizing. He finds it nothing short of annoying that teachers still use biblical texts in whatever way. What sense can this make to those who don't even know the stories of the biblical past? For a particular story which is being told at any time to contain even a fraction of the force the teacher intends, it is necessary that the listener know the whole range of the story. If men have not heard these stories in bible class or Sunday school, where shall they learn them? What is Easter without the story of Mary and

45

the gardener? What is Christmas without the Nativity stories in Matthew and Luke? What is Christian love without the good Samaritan and Lazarus and the rich man? Stories can be taught and learned; that is the task of Christin education. Van Buren wants the riches of both Testaments shared in extra-worship situations, so that when an attempt is made by the preacher-celebrant to make contemporaneous the reality of Christ he won't have to assume the whole didactic past.

Christian faith finds expression in language. It is expressed in other ways as well, both with respect to faith and to so many of man's concerns and activities. Language is one of the principal ways we have of communicating with one another. Believers when speaking as believers have said all sorts of peculiar things. They have said, "Jesus is Lord." They have said, "Glory to God in the highest." What can it mean for modern congregations to "thank God for His great glory"? Believers have said, "I believe in the Holy Spirit and in eternal life." But believers have also spoken as ordinary men in ways which do not particularly seem to express Christian faith. In saying such things as "Lyndon Johnson is president," "Three cheers for the Yankees," "I believe in the graduated income tax and old age pension," they seem to be uttering sentiments that bear no important relation to the former set of affirmations. Is it because the second set is about concrete things and persons which all of us, or many of us, care about, whereas the former have to do with another world?

I know Lyndon Johnson is our president. Do I know that Jesus is Lord? In each case, *how* do I know it? What kind of Lord am I talking about? These questions indicate the task of Christian education in serving faith, clarifying the relation between faith and knowledge. Van Buren is convinced, as the Catholic is, that faith is a kind of knowledge. He says we go a Christian lifetime without examining what kind of knowledge faith is. What is a fitting faith-proposition? How does the thoughtful man express the knowledge he has of Christian faith?

46

Must we just keep repeating those faith phrases forever without taking the pains to examine them? Without casting any aspersions on those ancient formulas, we must say that they did the job *once*. That is not to say that they are not doing it today or that they cannot do it today. It simply points up the fact that we very much need to know whether they are adequate to the needs of today.

Since what has been called in contemporary theological circles "the death of God" and the rise of critical historical imagination, writes Van Buren, Christians have had to find analogies for the objects of faith in new myths, stories, and parables. They have always had to do this, but before "the death of God" they could always pretend that their myths somehow gave them an insight into ultimate truth. Human love provides human faith with its most helpful analogy, and in this sense those engaged in Christian education have the task of teaching about faith.

The above paragraphs, I think, are a fair representation of the position taken by many who are giving serious thought to how Christians communicate that ultimate reality which is God.

There is another approach to the problem which must be considered seriously. This stream of thought is represented by Karl Barth when he says that men like Van Buren are making a grave mistake in their insistence on the need to accommodate the Word of God to the needs of men. We do not improve on the Word of God, we do not contribute to it, we do not clarify it. We must listen to it attentively or we will fall under its judgment. We try to measure up to the Word that is being spoken to us. This was the whole theme of Barth's lecture series in the U.S. a few years ago, which appeared as *Evangelical Theology*. What we must do as preachers and teachers is avoid muffling the Word's clear tone. God speaks to us; our hearts are either open to this Word of His or they are not. He speaks in tones of the loving instruction He has given to His people since the days of Abraham. We are the people formed by that Word. His message is not difficult to understand. He tells us this in Deuteronomy (30, 11–14). His message is near to us because He is very near to us. "Choose life . . . by loving the Lord your God, heeding his voice and holding fast to him" (Dt. 30, 19–20). There is no question but that we can be confused over God's Word to us if our minds are clouded and our hearts obtuse. We are sinners, and that makes it hard to hear God's Word. We can be prisoners of old ways and call them God's ways, when in fact they are only human ways we have grown accustomed to.

Christ speaks God's Word to us. This message of the Master goes unchanged. There are no absolutely sure human situations. Love requires true settlements which often give the appearance of compromise. But the Word of God received in faith is living; it is life-giving. We may not consider it to be the total Word of God when we receive it in any one form. We cannot speak or hear God's Word in an Eastern form or Western or European or Caesaro-Papist as if we were dealing with it ultimately.

To believe is to give one's person over to the person of God the Father. It will always be a question whether we have really said anything in phrases like the one just spoken. Ludwig Feuerbach says in *The Essence of Christianity* that the leaf on which a caterpillar lives is a world for the caterpillar. What God is to me, that He is. I cannot know what God is in Himself or for Himself other than what He is for me. If God were an object to the bird He would be a winged eagle. The bird knows nothing higher, nothing more graceful, than the winged condition.

Barth has an introduction to *The Essence of Christianity* in the Harper Torchbooks edition in which he essentially disagrees with Feuerbach but helps us by noting why this important book turned the tide toward acceptance of the formula, "God is man and man is God." Feuerbach has only one argument in that book; it appears in every chapter, but without inducing tedium.

It is this: the ideas of God and of every Christian mystery are shown to be nothing other than projections of human thought. God was made by man, Feuerbach maintains, and in fact is man.

The problem that faces the teacher of Christian faith is to make sure that what we call faith in God is not simply the projection of a Being in our own image and likeness (including some of the limitations which surround our being). We constantly speak the words of faith to hearers who presumably have the gift of faith, in a language of symbol which at one time stood adequately for the ultimates, Father, Son and Spirit. The readings in the lectionary of the Roman rite for the first Sunday after Easter provides an example of this. The first reading is from 1 John 5 and the second is from the twentieth chapter of John's gospel. In the first, John says that the blood and the water from Christ's side is a stream in which the spirit of God flows freely. The water of baptism flows in the Church; so does the blood of the eucharistic cup. The spirit gives life to both flowing streams. The writer is saying to his hearers: "You have the experience of Christian baptism. You have experienced in the eucharist drinking the blood of Christ. It is the spirit that enlivens both. These three, water, blood, and spirit, witness to the truth we teach."

That is the argument we find in the Johannine epistle. It is what we must preach on. We have to make it clear in Nanticoke, Pennsylvania, and Wa-keeney, Kansas, that water, the blood, and the spirit are three simple and easy signs by which Christ lives in our midst. The appeal made is to the sacramental experience of the community. It says, "You have the experience of God in faith, do you not? You come together to celebrate the holy signs which afford you that experience. What more compelling testimonies can I propose to you than these three, which are realities of your weekly existence?" The argumentation is all quite circular. It runs: faith is testified to by the behavior of a community of faith. What Christians do is the clearest sign of the Father, Son, and Spirit who cannot be seen. God gives these signs—the sacramental experience of the community—and through them we proceed to the certitude that He is behind them.

The gospel reading for that first Sunday after Easter is quite the same in its intention. The evangelist is speaking of those who have not seen and yet have believed. We have a problem as believers, and it is the problem of finite signs in this civilization which stand for the infinite, triune God who is not seen, among us who have faith in Him. I have not manufactured the problem. I may not have spoken of it clearly enough. But if you do not recognize the problem, then in an important sense you have nothing to say either to adult Catholics at Mass or to nine-year-old children. It is the problem of faith and symbolic signification.

You undoubtedly know something of the solutions proposed by St. Paul to this problem, and again of Bultmann and Bishop J. A. T. Robinson who is simply the popularizer of Tillich and Bonhoeffer, or of Bishop James E. Pike who is the popularizer of Robinson. The latter, in his sermons at Grace Cathedral in San Francisco, now collected in a book, says that the word "trinity" represents an illusion. Pike is not an original thinker but he has read enough of Bultmann and Tillich to be able to say that the word "trinity" does not mean much to modern man. It testifies, he says, to a conceptualization which in fact we are not capable of. In using that word we are employing an ideogram that falls far short of the reality of God. We are betraying the reality of God by saying He is a "trinity of persons." Since He is wholly other than we, we cannot describe Him as someone like ourselves, saying that He exists in persons and that there are three of them.

We who hope to be preachers and teachers have known since our philosophical studies that there is the problem of analogy. We take God in only by symbols of Him; we cannot know Him as He is. We know Him through our limited but somehow adequate idea of Him. To arrive at this cognition we use the symbols which He Himself has provided, symbols such as the cosmos. Our faith is a symbol of God at a higher level than that of the universe; so is the language in which we express our faith, and the language in which the scriptures are expressed. All are symbols of God. They stand for Him with sufficient accuracy and approximation that we may affirm our genuine conviction that we believe in Him and not in the symbols. In Feuerbach, the caterpillar can never get off the leaf. The Christian is forced to say that caterpillar-man lives on a leaf. But is God, for that reason, to be made the Great Caterpillar on a transcendent leaf? The minimum condition of holding fast to, and expressing, Christian faith is the conviction that we can proceed legitimately somehow from finitude to infinity.

The one thing that can always make that transition credible—that can even demand it—is the mystery of interpersonal human relations. There is no better sign available to us in the heavens or on earth than two human beings in a relationship of love. The sole problem of religious education, one might say, is that of helping people, adults and children alike, to regulate their love lives. This means that religious education consists chiefly in providing an experience of love. If it is Christian love it will necessarily be divine, which is to say human love transformed, carried out beyond itself to the Other.

4.

WHAT ABOUT THE DUTCH CATECHISM?*

WITHIN THREE YEARS after the adjournment of the Council of
Trent in 1563 a team composed of Dominican friars and secular
priests, the former theologians and the latter humanists (called
on to render the Italian original into Latin), produced a volume
for clergy entitled *Catechismus Romanus*. It was written in prose
form in four parts—faith and the creed, the sacraments, the
decalogue, and prayer—and was accompanied by copious mar-
ginal references to the Bible, the writings of the Fathers of the
Church and the *Summa Theologiae* of St. Thomas Aquinas. An
appendix to this volume, which shortly came to be known as
"The Catechism of the Council of Trent," correlated its contents
with the Sunday Epistles and Gospels of the Roman Missal. The
intention of this scheme was a continuing catechesis of Catholics
at Sunday Mass under the four headings listed above. The catechism was an extremely sophisticated book which reflected with
perfect fidelity the teaching and legislation of the recently com-
pleted Council of Trent. It has been extremely effective ever
since, and even though not many teachers of religion alive today
have examined it with any care, it nonetheless put its stamp on
every age down to 1960, the eve of the Second Vatican Council.

The bishops of Holland last year published a similar volume,
giving it the title, *De Nieuwe Katechismus*. It has appeared in
English dress in autumn of this year entitled *A New Catechism:
Catholic Faith for Adults*. It can very well stand as the catechism

* First published in *U.S. Catholic*, December, 1967, 6–10.

of this Council which was so much influenced by the theologians of the Low Countries—Belgium more than Holland—and so little influenced by the Roman theologians. The book is splendid in every way, a compendium of Catholic faith worthy of our times. It is described within its covers as the work of a team at the Higher Catechetical Institute, Nijmegen, "in collaboration with numerous others." The head of that Jesuit center is Father Willem Bless, S.J. No names appear on the title page. A brief foreword is signed "The Bishops of the Netherlands." The *imprimatur* for the original Dutch edition was given on March 1, 1966, by Cardinal Bernard Alfrink, and appears in the English translation. According to the publisher a first press run of 75,000 copies was produced, of which 30,000 had been sold to four Catholic book clubs before the book appeared.

The book is beautifully translated into English by Kevin Smyth. This is more than fortunate, for if the rendition were badly done the pain for the English-speaking reader would be acute. The book never falls below a level proper to clear exposition, and at times in its English dress it reaches lyrical heights.

By this time the reported adventures of the catechism at the hands of certain Vatican officials are well known. A news dispatch in the *New York Times* for August 2, 1967, reported a story in the Roman daily *Il Messaggero* to the effect that "Vatican sources" had discovered in the book no less than "ten major heresies and forty-eight minor ones." Much was also made of a reported meeting at Gazzada in northern Italy in January of this year between three curial cardinals and three Dutch theologians. By this time, the record of the Italian minority at the Council is so abundantly clear that whatever certain of its representatives define as Catholic faith may almost be taken for its opposite, and vice versa. Their concept of "heresy" seems to be whatever they do not understand or, understanding, cannot accept. The Dutch theologians of last January's meeting are quoted as saying tactfully that the differences between them and the Roman churchmen are chiefly in the areas of wording or expression; changes will be made involving rephrasing only, not content. The theological onlooker who is not at the moment the object of the zealous attention of "Roman authorities" is prone to say that the basic difficulty is that they do not recognize Catholic faith when they read it described in its fullness, in Dutch or any other language.

The catechism is above all modern. This is not to say that it is novel or contains any departures from the ancient faith. This it simply does not do—though it departs from some theological conventions which have erroneously been taken for the ancient faith. The book's concerns are those of contemporary man, especially in the first of its five parts, entitled The Mystery of Existence. The authors show themselves perfectly attuned to the insecurities and anxieties of our generation, while at the same time they show an awareness of modern certainties brought about by the scientific spirit. The book is most sure of itself when it is describing the condition of modern man in his world—whether man the believer or man the unbeliever. Paradoxically, it grows mildly tedious when it is describing the celebration of the Christian mysteries in the framework of the present liturgical year. This it does, generally speaking, after a treatment of a particular mystery in the earthly or glorified life of Jesus. The exegetical considerations put forward in support of a discussion of the New Testament text are always based upon scientific Scripture study, if perhaps on the conservative side in the spectrum of Catholic scholarship. They also contain insights which can only be described as fresh and life-giving.

The progress attempted from the meaning of the New Testament to its celebration in the life of the Church frequently, as we have said, gives the appearance of retrogression. The contemporaneous quality of the word of Scripture in the life of modern man is lost as an explanation is given of how that meaning is acted out in the cycle of the Church year. This is not to suggest that no liturgical celebration befits modern man, but only that he is badly served by the liturgical framework he now has in East and West.

At one point the authors of the catechism are at pains to point out that Christianity is not merely a matter of religion understood as ritual observance, and that the Christian mysteries are not tied to the forces of nature and the seasons. They illustrate this by pointing out that summer and winter come to the southern hemisphere when the northern hemisphere is experiencing exactly the opposite seasons. The effect of this observation is to help the reader know how irrelevant much of liturgy is to a Church that presumes to be universal. It was composed by and for men of a certain restricted segment of the earth's surface and becomes daily less useful to us as we become more global and less Mediterranean in our outlook.

Understandably enough, the central figure in the catechism is Jesus Christ. A section of 39 pages, Part 2, The Way to Christ (divided into The Way of the Nations and The Way of Israel), prepares for the extended treatment of Part 3, entitled The Son of Man. The latter portion continues for 134 pages and contains an extensive interpretation of the contents of the New Testament. The theological developments of the patristic era, the history of the Church down to our own times, and all of Christian life and morality under the aspect of sacramental existence are dealt with in Part 4, The Way of Christ (261 pages). The fifth and concluding part, The Way to the End (36 pages) speaks of old age, death, and man's hope which is fulfilled in God.

The telling of faith's story in this volume never grows dull, though at times it will be very familiar to a person whose work is in the theological field. Seldom does one find oneself wishing to vote differently from the authors in a matter of free choice in the realm of scholarship. They are at their most brilliant when they are seemingly farthest from standard "religious considerations." This is another way of saying that they have achieved a remarkable synthesis of Christian revelation and human life. Specific facts of sacred history or matters of simple fact in the life of the Church are reported fully, but one's interest does not quicken until one observes how a great contemporary question like the cosmic evolutionary process, or universal human guilt, or the meaning of man's freedom is dealt with by these authors. They are if anything conservative in their theological positions as in biblical matters, in the sense that they report dutifully on any theological construct that has long been held or can still be held by anyone who claims respectability in theological circles. They have a genius for reporting without comment a matter that has long flourished in the life of the Church, let us say since Augustine's time, but which is headed for obscurity in today's world.

The authority of Jesus Christ is almost the sole one resorted to in these pages. Citations from papal utterances do not occur. There will be an occasional phrase from Kierkegaard, Shakespeare, or Newman. The English edition contains a love poem by Hilaire Belloc—not an especially good one. In the extended treatment of gospel materials only one scholar's name appears and that by way of citation of his views, two or three times. He is Günther Bornkamn, a contemporary German Protestant theologian. Bornkamn is cited at one point in support of the reality of Christ's resurrection.

Jesus is described unequivocally as the way we know what God is like. The authors of the catechism do not discount the possibility that philosophy or moral sense or intuition may contribute to a knowledge of God. They are at ease in indicating at some length the ways in which Hinduism, Buddhism, and the teachings of Confucius and Lao-Tse lead to some knowledge of God through their concern for the fate of man. Nonetheless, Jesus is spoken of in more than one place as the fullest expression of the reality of God that has ever been made to man. The

56

catechism is almost harsh on any heretics of the past (e.g., Arians, Monophysites), or Catholics of the present, who presume to say aprioristically what God should be like, followed by a judgment as to how Jesus does or does not come up to that standard. The Dutch authors are fully evangelical and fully Catholic in maintaining, with the Savior and the apostles, that from a human point of view—the only one we possess—He himself is that standard. All convictions about the characteristics of God and His meaning for man are modified by the person of Jesus.

Among the treatments that are especially fine are those that deal with the way in which God can be glimpsed through one's loved ones; the treatment of dogmas as not mere words but values which enlarge our horizons; the treatment of the Christological councils—Ephesus, Chalcedon, III Constantinople, which are much discussed nowadays—as being concerned with the whole future of man and not simply verbal formulations, since nothing less than man's humanizing and his divinizing were at stake; and the treatment of the gospel miracles, never punitive, and always corresponding to faith rather than being contradictory of nature.

The sections on answers to prayer are especially helpful. There it is pointed out that despite the tragic termination of Jesus' earthly career, His prayer to His Father that the kingdom should come was in fact answered in His glorification. The treatment of the binding force of the transcendent counsels proposed by Jesus in the Sermon on the Mount is likewise good, as in the insightful comment which points out how enduring over the ages the norm "as oneself" has proved with respect to love of neighbor.

Jesus' favorite title for himself, "Son of Man," is featured as a divine title beginning with its origins in Daniel 7, while the slow progress of the title "Son of God" in the primitive Church from generic status to specific is handled very well. The authors are perhaps needlessly impatient with the familiar usage "Our

57

Lord." They are quite right in regretting its status as a cliché, but they do not seem to attend sufficiently to its Pauline origins. At the same time they are probably wrong in their assumption that through this title a confusion with God the Father is possible in the minds of Catholics, most of whom scarcely know Him as "the Lord." The cavil of the authors doubtless has to do with their fear of Catholic folk piety centered around a one-person God who is, in effect, Jesus Christ.

It is almost impossible to overpraise the treatment of the "newness" of the risen Jesus. Full attention is given to the resurrection appearances. It is carefully pointed out that there is no reference by any of the four evangelists to Jesus' actually coming forth from the tomb, or to the effect His coming forth had on the guards. The catechism points out that it was not until the medieval period that artists presumed to depict Jesus' actual resurrection and the terror it struck in the soldiers who witnessed it; in doing so they attempted what the evangelists never tried. This book is much more favorable to the artistry of the gospels than to that of those presumptuous daubers. The inability of the disciples to recognize Jesus immediately in His resurrected state, the chasm between His glorified state and His former natural state in which He could be fully embraced, His new orientation toward His Father—all these things are put forward with a perfect delicacy to make clear that while the experience of the risen Jesus by believers in Him was an event of their human histories, it was not a happening of history exactly like the happening of His crucifixion.

Jesus' consciousness of His person and mission is very deftly dealt with in these pages. So are such matters as the meaning of His getting ready for His life's work in Nazareth, and of the details in the stories He told—for example, the book's quiet insistence that the parable called that of the Prodigal Son is above all else a story about a father.

The catechism is excellent in its appreciation of the values of

Islam and the religions of the East. The tone is never patronizing, yet the authors do not hesitate to point out what they think are failures to meet human needs in these religious traditions. This makes it all the more surprising to read, "Though the Church is built upon Israel, though Jesus, Mary, and the Apostles were Jews, the chosen people as a whole refused to enter the Church. Nonetheless, they remain the people of God's first call. Their existence comprises a mystery, of which we can feel the force in chapters 9 and 11 of the *Epistle to the Romans,* which was written by a Jew, Paul. . . . As the Second Vatican Council expressly declared, it is impossible to deduce from Scripture that as a people they are rejected and accursed."

Now, none of the above is false, but the tone is so concessive and the silence on what actually took place between the years 30 and 135 A.D. (the date of the uprising of Bar Kokhba) so massive, that the Catholic who reads it will continue to find the religious situation of the contemporary Jew mysterious without need. Mystery it was and is, but the statement "the people as a whole refused to enter the Church," as it stands is simply false. What can be demonstrated is that a polarization began to take place early between groups of Jews in various cities of the Levant on the question of whether Jesus was Israel's Messiah. Paul testified to this situation in a series of brilliant theological reflections, both in *Romans* and elsewhere. But "the people as a whole" have never had the whole message of Christ presented to them, either in the first century or at any time since. Those few who encountered the gospel in person did so in terms of a struggle over the nature of Mosaic observance which clouded the question of Jesus from the start. The Jews of any subsequent generation inherited the history of a polemic, never the person and words of Jesus as they were available to some in the gospel period. Any hint of the complexity of the question would have absolved the catechism authors of the charge of being offensive to the perceptive Jewish reader. Their opaqueness on the question

59

is related to their inability to see Israel's history and Scriptures in any light but one of preparation for Christ. One does not expect a full blown theology of Judaism, since no Christian theologians have as yet developed one. Nonetheless, one could expect with respect to Judaism something of the positive values the authors cite in Protestantism precisely as it has been isolated from Catholic life and thought. These values are puzzlingly absent. Contemporary Jews, so important to the Christian, exist nowhere in this book except as "still called." "As a people they are more closely related to salvation than any other." Correct, but a painfully inadequate statement of a present religious reality.

The treatment of the Christians of the Reform is much more satisfactory on all counts. Of them we read: "It is impossible to estimate the immense amount of goodness and holiness which the Reformation, even in what is most peculiarly its own, has to offer all Christianity. The Catholic Church cannot do without the Reformation." And in another place: "On closer inspection, it appears that the Reformers happily took more with them than the Bible. They took, for instance, part of a Church fellowship (that is, good men in the tradition of Christ) and also some authoritative oral tradition." The catechism affirms the full ecclesial status of the Churches of the Reformation ("Even as bodies they are not left without Christ, without his Spirit"), as it must, to accord with the teaching of Vatican II. At the same time, it does not envision reunion without tears, since the differences which exist are real and not imaginary. The authors situate these differences radically in the sacramental principle of Catholic Christianity, its "more firm belief" that salvation is embodied in the most ordinary things, "the bread on the altar, the voice of an assembly at Rome, the words of absolution," as contrasted with the Reformation's certainty that "God cannot be so palpably attained in the Church." The Catholic tradition on salvation is seen as more rooted in history, the Protestant more in the divine transcendence which is beyond history; the Catholic tendency is to rely on the goodness of humanity even though it has sinned, the Reformed tendency is to mistrust it because it has sinned. The frankness of the catechism on these matters is explained: "Men are not united by denying the existence of divisions but by overcoming them." A resolution of the differences, when it comes, will probably not take the form of the Roman Church's absorbing the Reformation. "We all have to evolve together, towards a new Catholic, that is, universal Church. This does not mean a Church where the wine of Christ's truth is watered down. But it means a Church where forms and opinions which are not essential will be transformed and remoulded." It is sobering to note that extended quotations such as these are being featured in newspaper reports on the catechism, so newsworthy is it that one communion should speak understandingly of another in an official, hierarchically-sponsored book. "We know that we never possess the truth wrapped up in a closed compartment. The times are always new, the Church must always seek further for God's view of the human world. The Bible is always full of new life. What we know as Catholics is that the direction in which we are going is right. The signposts are placed correctly. This is the confidence which we have in the Spirit who leads the Church throughout the ages."

If one were to inquire about the volume's finest feature, this writer would be prone to name its spirit of compassionate dialectic. Questions are really mulled over and argued in its pages. The best case is always put for any doubtful opinion which has had long or widespread currency. Whenever a resolution is attempted it will be from a position of weakness—at least, as the attempt at synthesis gets under way. This low-key presentation will inevitably be redolent of the divine mercy itself; it will reflect the universal will of the forgiving Christ to save. One can foresee heavy weather for any attempts at faith-propositions characterized by intransigence, whatever the force

61

of the logic behind them. The catechism is consistently on man's side, on the supposition that a merciful Father is on man's side.

The approach to questions of sin and love, to matters which center around the striving of the human heart and its failures, is especially admirable. "Sin makes the world less good. Where sloth reigns, the fields grow thistles and the dikes collapse. . . . A humanity in sin finds the world a heavy weight to bear. . . . The thistles and thorns are within man himself." "In a world of ascending evolution, sin is often nothing but the refusal to grow in the direction which conscience reveals." "To love means to go out of oneself. Hence it is something quite obviously 'not in our line.' We are afraid of it, both of love of God and love of man. . . . We are all beginners in love. Egoism and bad faith, the inhibitions of inner disabilities and immaturities, all make us men who have still to learn nearly everything. We cannot learn the lesson by overtense effort. The foolishness of the gospel is calm. All overanxiety is unevangelical."

The gentle counsel of the book is surely a strong feature. The tone is never homiletic, understood pejoratively. Whether the matter under discussion is how parents should react to an adolescent who stops going to Sunday Mass or how we should deal with someone who breaks faith or religious communion with us, the wisdom of Christ is ever-present. The full faith of the Church on divorce and remarriage, for example, is enunciated clearly—yet when it comes to those who remarry outside the Church, "we should never judge such people harshly." For a young person to leave the Church for a while may sometimes signify spiritual progress, when everything has become obscure to him. "Circumstances may have shrouded the visage of the Church so that the Church—and hence Christ—has become unrecognizable to him. . . . It is necessary that parents should have an increasing respect for what the child sincerely believes, even if they think it is wrong. In any case, a child who has 'left the Church' must never be shown the door."

performance perhaps than the author of these lines, put the matter well in the one personal address to their readers they allow themselves. It was because of the great power of grace, they say, that they were encouraged to write this book:

"Though they knew that some of the heritage of sin and aversion from God might be reflected in the text, they were still more confident that the forces of truth and grace which flow to them through mankind and the Church would work superabundantly in the pages before you."

That is a proper modesty, and a sufficient justification for any such work attempted in God's name.

5.

WHO SHOULD TEACH RELIGION?*

IT SEEMS TO ME that the problems in religion teaching are chiefly two: getting people into the work who really enjoy doing it, and overcoming the resistance to formal instruction in religion which we have managed to create in Catholics of all ages over the years. I do not suppose that the whole scheme of religious formation can be so marvelously improved that all difficulties will be eliminated; but I do foresee a day when we make fewer blunders of the kind we are now rather consistently guilty of making.

First of all, I am convinced that religion teaching—never an easy matter in the best of times—is more difficult than ever in our day. Not only is the age pragmatic, critical, and bent on every sense-satisfaction available. It is also in full revolt against patterns of religious practice and outlook which up until fairly recently it "bought," on the assumption that it had to under pain of divine sanction. This is true indiscriminately in the Catholic and Protestant milieux, I should think.

As to increasing the number of religion teachers who really enjoy their work, an early step is to increase educational opportunities in this line so that the numbers of those who are ill at ease because ill-prepared will decrease, or put positively, so that the number of skilled practitioners will increase. We are nowhere near a realistic approach to this problem. The deep com-

*Address delivered at the University of Notre Dame summer session, School of Education, July 25, 1967.

mitment we have to general education in the Catholic community—the conduct of all-day schools—has effectively seen to it that we have not been serious about the preparation of religion teachers. I see the antithesis or opposition between the two as irremediable. I think we cannot get good at religious education until, by and large, we get out of the business of general education. Even as I say this, I am convinced that many a well-prepared teacher in a secular discipline is immensely effective in conveying a Christian outlook to youth. In their teaching of math, French, and English they tend to be reasonably well-equipped professionals who convey their own commitment to a value scheme as they go about their work. In general, when they begin to teach religion formally they spoil everything. If we keep our schools open—as I assume we mean to at both levels—we could improve their apostolic effectiveness overnight by not teaching religion in them. We would resort to some other context entirely. The immediate benefits of this scheme would be the termination of religion teaching as an exercise in indoctrination to captive audiences—the character it now has in students' minds; the cessation of the greatest tension-maker in the Catholic school, namely the religion period for which many teachers have neither taste nor talent; and finally, an end to the field day which authoritarian, emotionally frustrated, censorious, and other types now have under the cloak of the Christian religion.

I am convinced that enough benefits would come if religion were not taught in our Church-related schools to justify the elimination immediately. The quality of formal religious education, wherever it was then carried out, would not improve automatically, but at least the stage would be set. Only people reasonably good at the work, and professionally prepared for it, would be allowed to engage in it. This might include some full-time Catholic school teachers, but they would be a crew effective in their moonlighting—say some 10 or 20 per cent of the total

67

instead of the present 85 or 90 per cent. They would have managed to get a second professional education the hard way. They would also be possessors of skills possessed by a minority, which they could exercise at professional rates. It seems to me that we can conceivably conduct good schools in secular subjects at non-competitive rates, but we cannot have good religious education until there is serious bidding for the services of a relatively small class of trained people. Gold corrupts, I know, and one does not get zeal for the gospel simply by offering attractive salaries. Nonetheless, our sins in this area have been so many and are of such long standing that I cannot see their being overcome except by some massive equalizing technique such as the creation of a class of fully professional teachers of religion.

It seems to me quite unrealistic to suppose that our present structures will bring us any notable improvement in the scheme of things; we will only fall farther behind. I am speaking of the pitifully small number of U.S. and Canadian Catholic teachers who do winter study in religious education at a professional level and even those additional thousands who do a summer course somewhere. Any new educational opportunity is to be welcomed, whether it be the Verbum Divinum Centre in London, Ontario, or the University of Notre Dame's planned new sequence in catechetics in the department of education. Yet to me, all seem to be new bailing devices for a vessel which has a gaping hole stove in its gunwale. I am proposing a radical means— *the* radical means—to repair the hull. I have only a moderate interest in the various new bailing devices, having helped in the development of one of the more effective ones—efficiency up to 1.87 per cent. I mean the Catholic University of America's department of religious education, summer session.

The people who really enjoy the work of religious education are those who are ready for it. They tend to be people who know that the venture of faith is attended by risks; hence they are a risky crowd, by any establishment standards. If they are religious brothers and sisters they tend to be more likely to drop out of their congregations than to stay, and if they are priests they are likely to be mavericks in their diocese or religious society. This is because study of the gospel in depth has consequences—none of them fully predictable by those who launch on it in full earnest. Yeast makes the dough rise. The well-trained religion teacher—and I mean the intelligent, prudent one—tends to be yeasty. He tends to put Christ and the gospel before formalisms of any sort, including those of his own life-situation. The happy religion teacher asks questions. He encourages students to ask questions. People who ask questions make other people unhappy. The net effect on the religion teacher is that there are ways available to diminish his happiness. He is not a deliriously euphoric creature living in a dream world. But he likes his work, and when he is unhappy he is unhappy over the right things.

I have already proposed what seems to me the best means of reducing resistance to religion teaching. Needless to say, another voluntary scheme will have to be set up, but it will be a baby with some chance of survival, not the present CCD scheme. It will not be a matter of costly duplication. The present scheme could not possibly be more costly than it is, at least in terms of its effect on people's lives. Even though the message of Christ originates with God himself, the fact is that it only comes to men by way of personal invitation.

I will not discount the fact of the gospel's having been tied in with the life of a people, a tongue, a culture. This has been a fact from time immemorial, notably in ancient Israel. In our time, however, there is the unique opportunity to set faith free from complicating cultural factors: to make it a genuinely free option. The young resist strongly the monopolistic character of Catholicity as it is presented to them. They want to see it as something that can be chosen for or against on its own merits. To be sure, there is a good amount of youthful nihilism abroad

—dissatisfaction at anything that would curb complete self-expression and self-satisfaction. Granted all this. But the gospel is simply not something that is forced on anyone, and we are deep in the business of forcing it. In this, youth has all the best of the argument. Religion must become a demand item—not something everywhere available, not Bonhoeffer's "cheap grace."

This brings me to my last point, namely how I would like to see religion taught, on the supposition it was being done by people who enjoyed the work and did it in a good set of structures. The chief thing that needs mastering, I should think, is some sort of understanding of the precise difference Jesus Christ makes. He does make a difference. That is why we are Christians. But what that difference is is elusive, and we tend not to know it. We have worked out an elaborate nature-grace scheme, a two-level universe, the practical effect of which has been to make us misprize creation. We are almost totally disarmed for the current secular-sacred conflict because we have plumped so vigorously for the religious or the sacred as more or better—"supernatural" —hence, by definition, an extra, an addendum. We need to recover the notion, if we ever had it, of faith in Christ as the healing and reconciling and accepting of all that is true in human life. Despite all alienation, all bruising or maiming, life is a good, and one to be prized. We may not forget this. But indeed, we have forgotten it. Our Christianity has built foursquare on a misprizing of the culture, the times, even of the human. What our religion teachers need to be is a class of men and women thoroughly at home with the sources of faith, who then teach life; experts in theology, who do not teach theology; men and women fully conversant with the difference Christ makes and the Christ who makes the difference.

The master-work of creation is the redeeming of all mankind. It is an invisible work, like the mustard seed, like the yeast in the dough, like the seed growing silently. It is God's doing, not man's, and the marvel of it is that the outcome is so incommensurate with the early beginnings.

This work is the reforming of humanity through its informing by the Spirit. It is not a grafting on, a new construct, an addition, but a new reading of all human life, a true reading of all human life—man, the son of God become man his beloved son.

6.

ON EDUCATION IN ECUMENISM*

I SHOULD LIKE TO PREFACE my remarks with a fairly extended quotation from a book published by D. H. Lawrence in 1922, the year he came to America for a three-year visit. The book is entitled *Studies in Classic American Literature.* Lawrence is speaking of James Fenimore Cooper's romanticized version of the friendship between Natty Bumpo, the White Man, and Chingachgook, the Great Serpent, the Red Man. He describes the closeness between these two as a wish-fulfillment myth.

Certainly, if Cooper had had to spend his whole life in the back-woods, side by side with a Noble Red Brother, he would have screamed with the oppression of suffocation. He had to have Mrs. Cooper, a straight strong pillar of society, to hang on to. And he had to have the culture of France to turn back to, or he would just have been stifled. The Noble Red Brother would have smothered him and driven him mad.

So that the Natty and Chingachgook myth must remain a myth. It is a wish-fulfillment, an evasion of actuality. As we have said before, the folds of the Great Serpent would have been heavy, very heavy, too heavy, on any white man. Unless the white man were a true renegade, hating himself and his own race-spirit, as sometimes happens.

It seems there can be no fusion in the flesh. But the spirit can change. The white man's spirit can never became as the red man's spirit. It doesn't want to. But it can cease to be the opposite and the negative of the red man's spirit. It can open out a new great area of consciousness, in which there is room for the red spirit too.

* First published in *Experiments in Community,* The Liturgical Conference, Washington, 1968, pp. 23–30.

72

To open out a new wide area of consciousness means to slough the old consciousness. The old consciousness has become a tightfitting prison to us, in which we are going rotten.

You can't have a new, easy skin before you have sloughed the old, tight skin.

You can't.

And you just can't, so you may as well leave off pretending.

Now the essential history of the people of the United States seems to me just this: At the Renaissance the old consciousness was becoming a little tight. Europe sloughed her last skin, and started a new, final phase.

But some Europeans recoiled from the last final phase. They wouldn't enter the cul-de-sac of post-Renaissance, "liberal" Europe. They came to America. They came to America for two reasons:

1. To slough the old European consciousness completely.

2. To grow a new skin underneath, a new form. This second is a hidden process.

The two processes go on, of course, simultaneously. The slow forming of the new skin underneath is the slow sloughing of the old skin. And sometimes this immortal serpent feels very happy, feeling a new golden glow of a strangely-patterned skin envelop him: and sometimes he feels very sick, as if his very entrails were being torn out of him, as he wrenches once more at his old skin, to get out of it.

Out! Out! he cries, in all kinds of euphemisms.

He's got to have his new skin on him before ever he can get out.

And he's got to get out before his new skin can ever be his own skin.

So there he is, a torn, divided monster.

The true American, who writhes and writhes like a snake that is long in sloughing.

Sometimes snakes can't slough. They can't burst their old skin. Then they go sick and die inside the old skin, and nobody ever sees the new pattern.

It needs a real desperate recklessness to burst your old skin at least. You simply don't care what happens to you, if you rip yourself in two, so long as you do get out.

It also needs a real belief in the new skin. Otherwise you are likely never to make the effort. Then you gradually sicken and go rotten and die in the old skin.

The only genuinely common ventures in religious education that I have heard of, in which Catholic and Protestant or Episcopal children are receiving formal instruction jointly under joint auspices, are in one southwestern state and in one city in New England. An early step in the work of ecumenical religious education is the improvement of textbook material used by the various churches. Progress is being made in Jewish-Christian relations—for example, in the Roman Catholic series for elementary school use, *Bible, Life and Worship,* and the secondary school series *Roots of Faith.* I do not know anything comparable in Roman Catholic-Protestant relations, probably because we are much closer cousins, or better, brothers who fell out, and as a consequence find it harder to be reconciled than friends or distant relatives would. The differences in the liturgical rites between the Eastern and Western church *are* dealt with in Roman Catholic materials, but almost invariably from the angle of the Eastern-rite Catholic churches. This fact—given the phenomenon of the nine-hundred-year separation of the parent bodies of those churches—is putting the cart before the horse. When Eastern Orthodoxy is dealt with in Roman Catholic materials, it is generally done in terms of the "schisms" of Photius and Cerularius: 1054 and all that. Parenthetically, we have not nearly reached the stage in the Roman Church where we can discuss the painful problems of Eastern Catholicity in the U.S. It is a nationalism, or rather several distinct nationalisms. There are the problems of the old world in America, of ethnic and language traditions equaling the true faith, and so on. The reason Western-rite Roman Catholics cannot discuss these problems freely is that nationalisms are a fairly lively phenomenon in their own segment of church life, as I gather they still are in the Lutheran and, to a lesser degree, the Reformed families. One never sees a frank discussion in Roman Catholic textbook materials of the thorny question of national parishes or Eastern-Western bitterness within our Church. The assumption always in possession is that the *res catholica* is supreme in the Roman Church. Most of our time is spent making the point in a concessive, though not in a grudging, spirit that the Eastern expression of Christianity is fully legitimate: that these Catholics really have the body of the Lord at Mass, and that their priests are real priests even though married. (I might say, parenthetically, that in earnest Western attempts to arrange Eastern celebrations for Western children and adults to partake in, the defensive spirit of the East—understandably enough—often comes to the fore. Either everything Eastern is better because older, or else a spirit of allegory in explaining liturgical rites, which originates with the Eastern fathers, is pressed hard, a spirit which we of the West hope went out with Amalarius of Metz. In other words, the need for liturgical reform in the East is seldom assumed. This reaction is thoroughly understandable in light of all that Eastern Catholics [and Orthodox] have suffered at Western hands.)

Let me mention two books I have found helpful in religious education on the subject of ecumenism. If the materials they contained were available in Roman Catholic or Protestant textbooks, things would be much improved.

Sylvan Schwartzman of Hebrew Union College in Cincinnati is the author of a textbook which has extended sections on the genius of Roman Catholic and Protestant Christianity, and a briefer treatment of Eastern Orthodoxy. The expositions are done with absolute fairness. Their whole intention is to inform; no polarization with Judaism is attempted. Luther Harshbarger and John Mourant of Pennsylvania State University have in preparation a college textbook which is a model of fairness in exposing the various religious traditions of East and West in depth. Paradoxically, it is weak in its discussion of preaching as a means of transmitting faith, but it is strong in its attention to rites of worship as central in the life of Judaism and Protestant and

Roman Catholic Christianity. The book contains an especially good treatment of the revised Roman rite of the Mass.

The Roman Catholic pattern in textbook materials used to be simply to describe men and movements as schisms and heresies, schismatics and heresiarchs. We have had our decades of invective and opprobrium, now largely over, but we have not arrived at a period of full understanding, let alone appreciation of each other. One symptom of our failure to cope with the modern realities of the ecumenical problem is that we continue to deal with church differences in the arena of the past. There is little contemporary about our concern. You find almost no treatment of the United States Protestant Churches or the World Council of Churches as they now are. Our better classroom teachers do well enough through their access to the movements of Pope Paul, Archbishop Ramsey, Patriarch Athenagoras, and Eugene Carson Blake in *Time* and *The National Catholic Reporter,* but genuine background information, in sources where the normal teacher is likely to come on it, is in short supply. In Roman Catholic circles the war against other Christians is largely over; there is an "era of good feelings." Still, there is not yet a sufficient flow of information about the beliefs and practices of fellow Christians or of Jews, nor is there generally a sufficient appreciation of the full legitimacy of ecclesial traditions other than our own.

Since a satisfactory theology of the Church is the last bastion to be taken in the entire ecumenical movement, we should not expect classroom educators to solve what worldwide councils, synods, and congresses have not yet achieved. We are making some progress in areas like that of scientific biblical study. There, practically speaking, there is no difference among members of the various Christian churches except such as comes from basic differences in world outlook (*Weltanschauung*) or ecclesiology. Our most appreciable successes in ecumenical religious education have been in the area of joint appreciation for God's written word—the refreshing discovery that at a level of love for the Scriptures we are all one church. Biblical fundamentalism is, to be sure, not yet dead everywhere. The challenge to demythologize the New Testament—whether partially or totally as radical critics like Bultmann demand—is not yet widely understood or received. What does exist is a central core of biblical faith and exegesis on modern critical terms which is surely the chief bridge or link between Roman and non-Roman Christians in our day. There is likewise some progress being made in the area of liturgics or sacramental worship: the discovery of the importance and significance of baptism to all Christians; the near universality of our eucharistic meal behavior; even the likenesses of contour of the great Protestant Western liturgies—Anglican, Evangelical, Reformed—all of them extremely close in spirit to the Roman, though frequently enriched by Eastern elements in a way we of the Roman Church have only just begun to do. But there is not much factual information available to teachers on these matters.

There is ecumenical progress in the area of Christian social action. Perhaps you know of the resistance of racist-type Catholics to the new Benziger series of elementary-school textbooks for likening Dr. Martin Luther King to Jesus. Books such as these help Roman Catholic children to appreciate the fact that the Spirit of Christ is to be found everywhere, and particularly among Christians of other persuasions than Roman Catholic. This is important because it is an application of Jesus' own principles of right faith in Him. "By your fruits you will know them," He taught, and "Lord, when did we see you hungry and feed you, or thirsty and give you drink?"

The real question is, not what is right for other Christians to do by their standards, i.e., according to the light of their consciences, but in what measure are their standards and consciences identical with ours? How much are they the Church in the very sense that we are the Church, not in some highly qualified sense which equivalently means we are not the same Church at all? There is such a thing as being ecumenical from a stance of superiority, being a great lover of and consorter with Roman Catholics or Protestants, the "other," while never really accepting them as being absolutely the same as oneself in brotherhood to Jesus Christ and membership in the one saving community through which alone the benefits of salvation come to us.

I know there are deep problems of faith and theology stalking my remarks. I am aware of the dangers of false ecumenicism, indifferentism, and folly, of imagining the unity of the Church as achievable without tears. I realize the need to give witness to the truth, as did the Savior himself, even though it should cost us our lives. Still, Christian religious educators need to have some faith in the "new skin" of D. H. Lawrence, lest they strangle or suffocate in their own. I mean, of course, the new and complete Church of Jesus Christ which none of us has ever lived in, the Church not only of the Spirit but also humanly embodied: in actual living persons, if not yet in self-conscious institutions. We need to have faith in that Church not only for the future but also as a reality of the present. We need to live in a larger, roomier Church of Jesus Christ—his brothers, his body, his bride—than most of us now inhabit; and immediately, but without the denial of what is now Church, and true Church, and Roman Church, and reformed Church, for each of us.

The question that needs asking, it seems, is: must religious educators wait for their church leaders, aided by their theologians, to solve all problems of New Testament faith, theology, and polity—orders, ministries, powers—before they begin to act as if they really were one Church with all other Christians in a transcendent but nonetheless true sense? I think the answer has to be no; that they must go on the assumption of Christian unity as a present reality if only because it is the Master's clearly expressed will, hence something no one wishes to go against. All who wish to obey God and his incarnate Son are of the Church of his Son by their very will to obedience. Their own sinfulness and disobedience of the present, the pride and posturing of their fathers in the faith in the past, are realities which cannot be ignored. The past cannot be undone; the present can only be reversed by humility and repentance and good theology.

Yet there is another present which is a reality, and that is the will to be one Church in absolute obedience to the Father. It is the disposition of all of us here, and we stand for thousands, even millions, who are absent. We know we are one Church of Christ, and nothing can make us two, or three, or sixty-three churches. We mean to act, in all matters in which we can without disobeying a biblical precept as we understand it or without offending our weaker brothers, as if we were one Church, since in fact we are. I should add that I think that intercommunion is the one piece of Christian behavior likeliest to cause widespread offense, and that it should be abstained from until some church-wide understandings have been achieved in this central matter. Nothing should keep us, of course, from hastening such understandings.

What I have said means that the religious educator is not only a practical ecumenist but also—since he is a teacher, hence a theorist by definition—a theoretical one. He must do and teach as if Christ's Church were one, even though badly sundered by sin and pride, and he a member of it. This puts a heavy burden on him if he is not absolutely sure of himself in history and theology. It also makes him vulnerable, if there are those who have spiritual authority over him who do not have his catholic outlook and reformed convictions (both lower case). Yet he must write his educational materials and engage in his educational and prayer activities as if Christ's Church were one for the reason that it is one, and is fated to see an even richer and deeper unity on condition it is faithful to Christ and prays in the Spirit and with the signs He proposed.

This means that differences among Christians and between

79

Christians and Jews will be kept in proportion; that likenesses, equally, will be kept in proportion. But true or right proportion consists in this: in remembering that differences come from sin and folkway and language, whereas identities are comprised by the Spirit and the Son and the Father; by water and blood and bread and oil; by charity and faith and mercy—in a word by the "weightier things of the law."

The ministries or services of other Christian communions may not be impugned; an over-facile theory of apostolic succession or legitimate laying-on of hands may not be pressed; an imperfect theory of "true and real sacrifice," whether pro or con, may not be made too much of. Bitter differences are kept alive for centuries by popular mis-education, whether pulpit or otherwise. The great backbone of education to religious prejudice is bad theology and bad history, or either discipline imperfectly digested.

The solvent of this rigid form of mutual distrust is a great charity, a great openness, and a constant stress on those things we hold in common.

This is not a desertion of principle or departure from the faith of our fathers. It is a courageous march in faith toward an unknown future where there is neither Jew nor Gentile, male nor female, bond nor free, Catholic, Protestant, nor Orthodox in their present recognizable forms, but only oneness in Christ who is all, and in us all.

7.

WHO IS READY TO TEACH THEOLOGY?*

WE WHO ARE HERE are engaged in a work that has several important presuppositions. The first one is that the Church has a stake in higher education. Mr. Harvey Cox says, "Get out of the university game. You can't play it well," but I am going to suppose that many of you think it is a game we should stay in, at least in some measure. Another presupposition is that the bulk of Catholic students who attend colleges conducted by the Church have the theological virtue of faith—Catholic faith. A third is that students who profess Christian faith may profitably study it on a theological level or in a theologically oriented way. Many of us think all three presuppositions to be valid, though one or other may hold a qualified position with respect to a particular one, a "*placet iuxta modum,*" as it were.

Members of this Society tend to have strong convictions about theology study by laymen who are receiving a higher education. We know or at least strongly suspect what the job is in this regard, and want to do it better. We find ourselves frustrated by factors that keep us from doing it better—sometimes even from doing it minimally well. We are faced with the delicate question of exploring the riches of the gospel seriously or "scientifically," as it is sometimes said, with young men and women so that they will grow in their knowledge and love of Christ—so that they will leave college firmer in faith and more

* Address delivered at the College Theology Society, New York regional meeting, November 20, 1965.

ardent in charity. We know that only the Holy Spirit can accomplish this, but are bent on discovering those means that will interfere least with His purpose.

It might be helpful to examine the total Roman Catholic situation obliquely, namely by way of the general American experience. The chief supposition on which U.S. colleges were founded was that, since the gospel was divinely revealed, it devolved on students to grasp its meaning along with their pursuit of humane and scientific studies. The founders of the infant institutions in the colonies were believers, and more usually ministers of the gospel. The populace was largely a Christian one; so were the student bodies. The culture assumed religion to be true despite major differences with respect to biblical interpretation, the trinitarian-unitarian conflict, and a never wholly absent deist or skeptic strain. Protestant and Catholic beginnings in higher education run largely parallel, with perhaps a difference in schedule of two hundred years. A notable difference is the change in the prevailing cultural assumptions as between the eighteenth, nineteenth, and early twentieth centuries and now, plus the fact of a renewal in the Roman Church and in the Churches generally in this age which has no exact parallel for as long as the American republic has existed.

The European university, medieval and Christian in its origins, is largely unfamiliar with the study of religion apart from its faculty of theology. Once a student has concluded his formal religious education in the state schools where there is a concordat, or in a confessional *lycée* or *Gymnasium,* his intellectual training in religion is at an end. He may continue religious practice at the university, but any synthesis between faith and reason in his professional or humanistic studies is his own doing by way of study circles, much as in the Newman situations in this country.

In the United States and Canada more ambitious attempts

have been made to provide studies in religion at the college level which, whatever the qualitative differences, is Europe's university level. The offering of courses in moral philosophy and Christian evidences was universal practice at a time when the colleges were conducted by the various Protestant churches. During that period the need for a learned ministry was so widely acknowledged that Hebrew, Greek, and even divinity studies were carried on with public moneys at the foundations which later came to be private and state universities.

The gradual retirement of Protestant groups from the administrative control of American colleges, and the increasing entry of the Catholic Church into the field, are facts fairly well known to you. Quite apart from the Catholic entry, a certain bitterness among churches and individuals marked the transition, for example that which obtained between the theologically fundamentalist and liberal groups. There were other important factors, of course. Among them was the growth in favor of the concept of college education with public funds. This necessitated the judicious conversion of many colleges from church-affiliated to non-sectarian status in order that they might qualify for land grant, Carnegie pension, and similar benefits.

In the present situation a number of state constitutions specifically—and, as many suppose, the federal constitution by implication—forbid the teaching of religion with public moneys. This has caused a few serious embarrassments in higher education circles. Not the least is the inability of college instructors to develop on even a modest scale certain great themes in literature, the fine arts, and history because students know nothing of the Bible or Christianity. A knowledge of post-biblical Judaism is positively esoteric, or would be if familiarity with the more widespread religious suppositions of the West—a knowledge of the Old Testament and the New plus the major Christian doctrines—had not merited the distinction.

Yet the question whether religion should be taught in the

state university is in some way entirely theoretical. It is being taught there in one fashion or another. To the question that immediately presents itself, "Legally?", most presidents and deans think they have an affirmative answer. A study done more than a dozen years ago by Seymour A. Smith, subsequently president of Stephens College, indicates that ninety-seven per cent of the state universities offered religion courses in some department, while in seventy state universities an average of nine courses in religion was being offered. Considerable confusion attends these efforts, it should be noted. Many of the courses are makeshift arrangements which fail to receive full academic recognition. Budget figures are frequently sub-par when it comes to financing religion courses. Deans affirm that such work is not always on an academic level with other disciplines, especially when clergymen are the instructors. Mr. Herman C. Wornom, executive secretary of the Religious Education Association, has reported that in extended visits to twenty state university campuses in 1955–57 the question most frequently put him by the deans and presidents he met—and already a selective principle was at work there—was: "How can we teach religion better? Where do we recruit the professors?"

There does not seem to be much debate as to whether the ultimate questions and concerns of man should be raised in the university classroom. Most agree that inquiry into man's destiny, the question of determinism vs. free will, the problem of pain, the meaning of the universe, are topics that have a place there. The question is: will a genuine search for truth take place or will unreflected answers testifying to belief or unbelief be provided students, on terms radically different from those of the rational, disciplined inquiry that goes on in the university classroom? Basically the question hinges on whether the men and women who hold religious convictions most earnestly are capable of giving them academic treatment.

84

You and I are proceeding on the assumption that we can be earnest, honest academics; that being a religiously committed person is not a disqualification. We should realize that this assumption of ours is distinctly a minority view. The precise form the problem takes in Catholic colleges is that only the person who could make the grade in a state university course in religious thought should be let try to "make it" in the Catholic college classroom. No one else need apply. Yet the Catholic course in college theology is crowded with teachers who could not so "make it."

John Stuart Mill framed the question in his inaugural address at St. Andrew's University in a way highly suitable to modern man. Mill asked, "Why should it be impossible that information of the greatest value, on subjects connected with religion, should be brought before the student's mind; that he should be made acquainted with so important a part of the rational thought, and the intellectual labors of past generations, as those relating to religion, without being taught dogmatically the doctrines of any church or sect?" Presumably teaching dogmatically to Mill meant teaching in doctrinaire fashion—simply presenting religious propositions "to be held" without any hint of how they first came to be believed or what their inner meaning is or their relation to the whole structure of human thought. Mill maintained that if men of good will and equal ability have come to the widest diversity of opinion on religious matters there is everything to be said for demonstrating how the variant results were arrived at.

This line of thought seems conducive to an impartial teaching about religion which is favored by many who are interested in state university education. The fair-minded academic person is not impossible to discover, it is maintained; far from it. Therefore let such a one describe the tenets of Roman Catholicism and Buddhism with exactness and sensitivity as he would those of Marxism if he happened to be on the political science faculty.

Some maintain that a professor of religious thought is more fitted to the task in proportion as he is not committed, for the reason that, unlike the thoroughgoing Communist, Quaker, or Catholic (who cannot but wish that his hearers should be of his persuasion), such a professor does not care. He wants comprehension in his students, not commitment. Intelligent dialogue or discourse is much more apt to be forthcoming from such teachers than from others, it is said, because they are as open to opposite positions as to the one they expound. Since the very essence of religious conviction is that all contrary claims are unconvincing to the one who believes, such claims are likely to receive from him either a hollow presentation or scant notice. But this situation is intolerable in chemistry or history, therefore it should be so in religion.

We Catholics know the phenomenon of one-sidedness in the form of listing "adversaries," demolishing absent heretics, nervously getting down to "what the Church holds" as soon as one can. Our students tend to resent many theology and philosophy courses because their instructors never seem to be fair to opposing views, nor do they even make sufficient attempt to understand them.

There exists in American society the paradox of academic freedom in every area of human inquiry except the theological, if certain philosophies of education are followed. In the religious realm our society has given the universities it conducts no clear mandate to engage in religious or theological discussion as part of their teaching function. The Church-related college has traditionally said that it exists to correct that omission.

The alternative described above of having the uncommitted expound the tenets and practices of the great religions dispassionately has been described by religionists as taking religious thought out of the hands of the trained men who might be presumed to know something about it and putting it in the hands of amateurs. Not so, comes the response. Need a man be successively a Platonist, Aristotelian, Stoic, Kantian, and Hegelian to teach a course in the history of philosophy? No more, then, need he be a Buddhist, Muslim, or Christian to deal with those great traditions at the level of rational dialogue. Once a clergyman or even an unordained expositor of his religion's scriptures is engaged for this purpose, however, his first approach to his religion will be non-rational commitment. As a corollary of his office, there will be the felt mission to win disciples.

The major barrier to religion study in the university is that the academic fraternity will not have it there because it is foreign to the understood terms of the pursuit of truth. The academic fraternity in the Catholic college maintains that it need not be foreign to these terms. We need to ask what these terms are so that we can determine whether the charge is true or false.

University terms are, quite simply, the communication of such understandings as the teacher possesses. He does not become better qualified in proportion to the measure in which the inner consistency of his discipline eludes him. He is not kept from strong views in his course; on the contrary, students rather expect them. A man does not become a bad economist because he is a Keynesian, or a bad exponent of literature because he follows the new criticism. He becomes an unacceptable academic man only when his economic or literary theory turns doctrinaire, that is, becomes a winnowing device to sift out any evidence that might tell against his theory.

One can conceive of a course in religious tradition which would be taught by a believer in that tradition with such fair-mindedness that no compulsory auditor would feel offended by anything but the compulsion that placed him there. The present resistance to the notion will allow courses in the psychology of religion or comparative religion without blinking an eye, but will forbid religious thinkers and theologians access to the classroom because they are so unmistakably committed to a view.

Departments of "philosophy and religion" exist in which no professor is clearly identified with a religious tradition, since it is supposed that such an identification is not a necessary condition of plumbing a tradition's deeper meanings.

The alternative to this state of affairs would seem to be to put the theologian in the theologian's chair; not the homilist, the shepherd of souls, nor the theological bully, but the theologian (or the master of religious thought in traditions which do not speak of a theology). This means a trained scholar who is fit for the work of college or university education. Not all graduates of theological seminaries are automatically disqualified as beginning teachers. After all, a theological education is provided in seminaries. Conceivably it could be a good one as well as a bad. A university education which will have provided some academic experiences outside of an exclusively theological or confessional milieu would seem, however, to qualify a person in a special way.

The college or university has been, from its inception, a little world of its own. It has its canons of deportment, its *lingua franca,* its scale of competencies which are precisely those that Church and family ordinarily do not have. When it asks those who expound theology to do so in terms of relevance to the lives of students it asks something legitimate. The university cannot require theology to abdicate its principles or methods, but it can ask theologians to present their discipline more in the manner of the liberal arts than as preparation for a profession, namely the ministry. (It may be noted parenthetically that Aquinas in his lifetime found no intellectual haven among the members of the faculty of theology of Paris. They accepted the friar only when forced to do so. The faculty of arts, contrariwise, was his champion in life and death.)

The dearth of laymen academically well-trained in theology or non-Christian religious thought provides a hardship to college and university administrators. In the Catholic case bishops normally cannot spare clergy except for pastoral purposes. The university takes the problem off their hands largely by not being interested in the priest-professor. It may welcome the Newman chaplain as a campus pastor; his privately conducted courses it has come to expect. But as an academic person he has not generally been sought out by the university, which will no more have him thrust upon it than a bishop will have priests thrust upon him by a zealous neighbor bishop.

Let us turn to the professional class that we ourselves comprise, in Catholic colleges by and large. We are men and women of religious conviction in an academic milieu that frequently does not share our conviction; I mean precisely the Catholic college. Some of us are ill-trained theologically, limited in our outlook, or narrow in our approach. But when as a class we call theology an integrating discipline we hope we are not trading shibboleths. When we say it we really mean it. Two important questions are, do we understand what we say, and are we sufficiently professional to achieve that integration?

I suggest that by and large we are too few for the task and generally unready for its challenge. I scarcely need rehearse the reasons, you know them so well. But let me name a few. The supposition that anyone can teach religion at college level is still a lively holdover from former decades. The presence of priests—who by definition are a non-academic class, though some of them do become respectable academics—in college education continues to be an unexamined fact of Catholic life. The victimization of religious brothers and sisters by bishops, and the bishops' own distress over filling chaplaincies in motherhouses and colleges, continues with only the slightest diminishment. The war goes on, in which the inability to pay suitable academic salaries and the use of religious personnel as economic hostages are the chief factors.

There are still rivalries among adjacent religious communities. Most often they are unconscious, non-acrimonious rivalries built on simple ignorance of the realities of higher education. The result is the careless planning and planting of new faculties—compounded by a thrust in the direction of the college education of the religious themselves, which might be a good thing if the education provided in such colleges were any good. There continues to be panic at the existence of municipal and area colleges where Catholic students will be imperiled in faith. There is still very little disposition to examine the proposition that the Catholic college can be even more harmful to the faith of those who attend it, not to speak of its possible deleterious effect on the whole body Catholic and American.

The condition of theological education in the Catholic community is pretty well known. It is not a healthy one. Numerous fears and anxieties have attended it and in parts of the community still do. Certain wrong theological positions have consistently been inculcated as demands of Catholic faith. The clergy by and large fear free and open inquiry in religious matters. They need a "right answer." Many are uncomfortable in the presence of multiple sources, multiple views. The preferred status of the "manual" continues, not the bad old manual like Pesch or Noldin but the new, single book that is a safe guide through the semester.

Permission to read what used to be called forbidden books, until the scheme lapsed into disuse, went on the assumption that a kind of moral turpitude attached to the request.

Often the mischief is made by the outlook of presidents, deans, and provincial superiors or bishops. Theology for them means safe catechetics or pastoral care. A service department is connoted. In it no major is contemplated; no distinction is made between the work of the upper division and that of the lower division; there is no option to take or not to take such work as one pleases. Often the administrator has had as much theological opportunity (or as little) as his theological faculty. He therefore has no respect for it, or if one of his professors comes to possess a theological competency he fears the difference. He may hire one genuinely trained person, or see to the doctoral education of one person, as a sop to his conscience. This overburdened individual is referred to immediately on all public and private occasions as proof positive of the seriousness with which theology is taken at the institution.

Consider, for a moment, the normal seminary situation. No one chooses to go to a Catholic seminary for scholarly reasons. Indeed, almost no seminarian can choose which seminary he will attend. There is no competition for academic posts on Catholic seminary faculties. No one's academic standing depends on his scholarly production. There has been until recently no freedom on the part of students to leave a seminary to attend a lecture, concert, or intellectual evening of one's choosing. The same is doubly true for one's theological training as a sister or brother, though this can later be remedied by study at a university faculty. The abortive multiplication of "sister formation" colleges, so-called, defers theological seriousness for at least four years.

Now all these factors lend an unmistakable tone to the theological enterprise we are in. We need to break through not only our own cocoon but that much thicker one in which those who guide our destinies are wrapped. There seems to be no way out of the situation except for teachers of theology in Catholic colleges, possibly through their professional association the College Theology Society, to make a massive exposé to the regional accrediting associations of their general unreadiness to do the job. We do not have much precedent for any such frankness of approach. But we could and should begin somewhere.

8.

RELIGIOUS STUDIES IN ROMAN CATHOLIC COLLEGES AND UNIVERSITIES*

THE U.S. ROMAN CATHOLIC college and university have been offering academic courses at the undergraduate level since the earliest days of these institutions in the latter nineteenth and early twentieth centuries. These academic courses, normally known as work in "religion," have been a degree requirement for all students, from the outset until very recent times. The progress of this movement is recorded in three studies done in the Department of Religious Education at The Catholic University of America in the mid-1950's by Simonitsch and Maher, and in 1963 by Carton.

At the very beginning, academic work in religion was offered on a once-weekly basis, whether with or without academic credit. The next development was to have it offered twice weekly, and during this period of expansion (between the 20's and the 40's) it was almost universally a credit-bearing study. The high point of academic requirement was reached around 1950 when large numbers of Catholic colleges demanded a course in religion for each semester of the student's enrollment. This was the situation for Roman Catholic students, at least, who normally had a degree requirement of sixteen credits and often enough a matching requirement of eighteen credits in scholastic philosophy. In

* First published by the Department of Higher Education, National Council of Churches, in *The Study of Religion in College and University,* New York, 1967, pp. 24–31.

general, such was the case with those who pursued the A.B. or academic B.S. degree. Students of education, engineering, nursing, and commerce frequently had a diminished requirement in both theology and philosophy. In a small number of cases all students in a given institution were held to the above requirements, with or without respect to their profession of Catholic faith, although the more usual case was that those who were not Catholics were held to the philosophy requirement, and in religion study were free to take the "Catholic courses" so-called, or to take other work in the study of religion specifically designed for those who were not Catholics.

The most grievous inequity in the scheme was the situation in those colleges where nothing in substitution was required of those students who were not Catholics, leading to occasional declarations on the part of academically hard-pressed Catholic seniors that they no longer professed Catholic faith. This "apostasy in the dean's office" has largely, but not entirely, been corrected by subsequent developments.

In 1955 there was held the first annual convention of the Society of Catholic College Teachers of Sacred Doctrine at Trinity College, Washington, D.C. Founding members of this group had spent the best part of the previous year laying plans for the Society's first meeting. The impetus came from interested parties in Washington, D.C. and New York, N.Y., including some seminary teachers who had devoted much of their summer time to instructing religious brothers and sisters who were college religion teachers. At the time of the founding of the Society, strong representations were made by the executive secretary of the National Catholic Educational Association, the Right Reverend Frederick G. Hochwalt, to the effect that a new professional group was unnecessary, since the College and University Section of his association was willing to entertain papers and discussions on college religion study at the annual national meeting and the various regional meetings. The founding members respectfully submitted the view that it was precisely because of the difficulties of dealing with this discipline adequately within NCEA structures that they were establishing the Society.

The sesquipedalian title of the new professional group resulted from a number of factors. The struggle of fifteen years ago in Catholic college circles centered around the use of the terms "theology" or "religion" to describe the academic enterprise of the colleges. In a most general way, the Dominican Fathers of the eastern and midwestern provinces, who at that time held many lectureships in Catholic colleges for women, besides staffing their own Providence (Rhode Island) College, were disposed to describe what they were doing as "theology," whereas the Jesuit colleges of the country and those conducted by nonclerical religious who were in good part oriented toward Jesuit institutions, were inclined to describe their departments as departments of "religion." This alignment of the mid-50's is a rough and general one. There were exceptions on both sides, in the sense that numerous colleges other than those described above were beginning to adopt the title "theology" in preference to "religion" in proof of the seriousness of their concern. In any case, the title of the Society was arrived at by compromise. It resulted directly from the discussion of the polyvalent nature of the term *sacra doctrina* found in the early articles of Aquinas' *Summa Theologiae.* Not long before the naming of the Society, the Reverend Gerald Van Ackeren, S.J., dean of St. Mary's College, St. Marys, Kansas (a Jesuit theological seminary), had published a doctoral dissertation at the Gregorian University in Rome exploring this term used by the thirteenth century Dominican friar to describe the content of sacred scripture, any theological synthesis built on biblical teaching, and the act of teaching itself.

The thirteen years of the Society's existence have seen numerous changes in this field of study in Catholic colleges and universities. Chief among them is a general improvement of the quality of theological education available to teachers of theology in college or those who have this work in prospect. There has been, first of all, the slow improvement of "pontifical" faculties of theology within the Roman ambit (this would include the Catholic higher faculties of theology, closely supervised as to their curriculums by Roman curial authorities, in the city of Rome, Canada, the U.S., Switzerland, Italy, Spain, and Latin America, but not so much in France, the Low Countries, or West Germany). Independent of this progress, which has been barely perceptible in some cases, there came into being in this country and Canada a number of M.A. and Ph.D. programs in graduate faculties of liberal arts designed for theological study by persons in the clerical, religious, and lay states indiscriminately.

The Catholic University of America had had such a program in its Department of Religious Education since 1938, which, in 1957, began to be oriented in the direction of Christian theology and religious thought. St. Mary's College, Notre Dame, Indiana, began a School of Theology for sisters and laywomen in the late 1940's. Marquette University, Milwaukee, began a vigorous master's program in 1958, and a Ph.D program some five or six years later. The University of Notre Dame began a winter M.A. sequence at about the same time as Marquette, although its summer session Master of Arts programs in theology and liturgy had been in progress for some time before that. Fordham University in New York had a graduate department of religion in its school of education from the 1940's. This became a program in religious education in the early 1960's, at about which time a department of theology came to birth in the graduate school. The first Ph.D. candidates at Fordham University and St. Michael's College of the University of Toronto were accepted four years ago, and those at the University of Notre Dame two years ago.

A distinguishing feature of these sequences was their acceptance of clergy and nonclergy on an equal footing for the

95

degrees indicated, St. Mary's alone comprising an exception. The instruction did not assume on the part of the students a familiarity with theological tag-lines in Latin, even though a knowledge of Latin was required for entrance into most of the programs. Much of the instruction was weak, in the early days of the pursuit of these degrees. Still, there was about the programs a spirit of theological openness and ecumenicity not generally found in the higher faculties of theology, which were thoroughly clerical in their student bodies and teaching staffs. It should be remarked, parenthetically, that some of the best theological instruction available in the early days of these theology departments in faculties of arts was provided by seminary professors. They not only gave generously of their time to a cause the importance of which they had come to see, but also welcomed the freshness of viewpoint represented by the hetero-geneous student body as contrasted with their own seminary student bodies.

While numbers of college teachers have earned the Ph.D. or S.T.D. degree (the latter the highest pontifical academic award) over the last dozen years in preparation for their work in the classroom, the existence of full-time, winter M.A. programs saw to it that the college theology classroom continued to be presided over in disheartening numbers by teachers with inferior theological educations. This M.A. degree was frequently avail-able after one year to those who had not been college theology majors. There was also the proliferation of summer session pro-grams leading to the M.A. after anywhere from four to seven summers of study.

The largest number of those who teach theology in the Catholic college continue to be priests with seminary educations who have not had the opportunity to do further study. It is sometimes remarked that the seminary was not helpful in making them pedagogues, but this does not comprise nearly the weakness afforded by the inferior quality of their theological educations in certain seminaries. Some of the best theology teachers in the Catholic colleges are priests with a seminary education only and nonclerics who hold master's degrees in this discipline by the summer route. These are noble exceptions, however. The fact remains that after thirteen years of the existence of SCCTSD (which changed its name to The College Theology Society in March, 1967) the profession of college theology teaching in Roman Catholic circles is not one that is academically at ease. Its inadequate preparation continues almost undiminished.

An early ideological difference in the group described above was between those who declared themselves committed to teaching for an intellectual end and those who maintained they taught for commitment. The terms of this argument were as incomplete in their disjunction in the Roman Catholic community as any place where it has been carried on. The "intellectualists" tended to be persons with a serious academic concern who had long ago discovered they did not have the gift of arousing commitment in students, and who had decided to settle—in the public forum, at least—for what they thought they could do, namely, propose an acceptable analysis and synthesis of the Christian mysteries. The "volitionalists" tended to be those who knew that religion was a way of life and not an edifice of ideas, but who at the same time tended to be ill-prepared themselves and somewhat belligerent over this fact. Both spirits are largely dead in the Society, the new synthesis being one of awareness that full intellectual seriousness is the best guarantee one can have that he is inviting any students to Christian commitment.

Meetings of the Society, both national and regional, continue to concern themselves with the problems of teaching, and the situation of the student who sits in a college theology class. Nonetheless, there is a widespread discouragement among college theology teachers because so many know they will complete a career at this work without ever having the benefit of a first-class theological education. Their class-loads and student-loads tend to run high, both because departments are frequently under-staffed and because the degree requirement in theology continues to remain high. The latter is true despite the fact that more and more colleges have converted to a three-credit scheme in theology, and the graduation requirement shrinks from sixteen to anywhere from fifteen to six hours. One college (Webster, St. Louis, Mo.) is on record and others are reported as contemplating dropping any courses required of all students.

Members of the profession in the Roman Catholic Church are sharply divided, it would seem, between those who wish to retain the fairly extensive requirement in college theology and those who would be pleased to see the religion department well staffed with trained persons offering courses in religion to those who elected them only, while at the same time offering a strong major in the field. About fifteen Catholic colleges in the U.S. offer a major in theology or religion study, at the present writing. Some of these are majors by a courtesy title only, in that there is not much course work available beyond the required courses and a few seminars and papers, whereas others—generally in colleges attached to graduate schools—will have as many offerings as do majors in other disciplines.

An important consideration is the relation between religion study in college and university to that in the seminary in the Roman Catholic community. Our seminaries increase in seriousness of purpose as academic institutions, many of them having sought state and regional accreditation for master's pro-grams offered in course to the better students. An important and inevitable difference between the seminary and the graduate school is that graduate schools are populated by students who opt for degree work after the bachelor's degree. This is generally a sign of intellectual concern if not necessarily of competence. The seminary, on the other hand, is populated by students whose primary concern is to become members of another profession than the learned profession, namely the priestly ministry. Not even the fact of high intelligence and scholarly habits in seminary bodies can alter the purpose of such institutions. They simply have no existence as graduate schools of religion in the Roman Catholic community. Many of their students feel a calling to the learned profession as well, as they go through the seminaries, and they engage in theological study in such a way as to ready themselves for more of the same, i.e., in circumstances that will prepare them for the college or university lecture hall. Nonetheless, the respective make-ups of the two student bodies constitute important differences in the approaches taken to sacred studies.

Another difference which is of no small consequence is that nonclerics who intend to pursue careers in the teaching of religion or theology are not to be found as fellow-students of Catholic seminarians during the important first four years of professional, post-collegiate theological study. The first exception to this on any large scale came in fall, 1967, when St. Mary's College, St. Marys, Kansas, began to comprise a School of Divinity along with the members of the Department of Theology in the arts faculty of St. Louis University. There, for the first time in the U.S., candidates for the Roman Catholic priesthood will take theological work in the same courses and classes as men and women students who are doing graduate work in theology. Something like this has long been the case at The Catholic University of America, where small numbers of seminary students have earned M.A. degrees in religion, in the graduate faculty of arts and sciences concurrently with their seminary studies, and even smaller numbers of non-clerical religious and lay students have studied with seminarians in the faculty of theology. This has been so infrequent an occurrence, however, that the eyes of the Roman Catholics of this country are on the beginnings, at St. Louis University, of what many are convinced will be the wave of the future. It is not supposed that all seminary students

99

will take their work in faculties that are "mixed" as to sex and professional concern. The all-male seminary which is a complete academic unit in itself, it is presumed, will continue in Roman Catholic circles just as in Orthodox and in Protestant. The fact remains, however, that interest in the study and teaching of theology widens among U.S. Roman Catholic laymen, sisters and brothers, chiefly in virtue of this Church's long-standing commitment to the teaching of Catholic faith in academic circumstances to college students. As a result large numbers of persons of every state in life will continue to be needed, so long as this commitment continues in some form.

Just as in the Protestant churches, enrollments in Catholic theological seminaries are decreasing, either through small entrance classes or through discontinuance in course. Up until a few years ago, former seminary students who seemed to have no special academic vocation were turning to graduate school departments of theology or religion, almost without examination of their own resources and interests. At the same time, of course, a number of very well equipped young men made this change from seminary to graduate school. The trend nowadays is in the direction of fewer making such a transfer as a matter of course. The increased selectivity of the graduate schools has much to do with this, plus the fact that only those former seminary students who are genuinely called to a life in the classroom seem to be seeking admission. Frequently such students will experience a brief hardship with respect to the ordinary ways of scholarship, if they have been enrolled in institutions where the lecture method in theology was featured. They will tend to be familiar with a "received theology of the schools" and not so well acquainted with contemporary theological writings, Catholic and Protestant.

A few arrive in the state of revolt against all that has gone before in their academic lives. Their knowledge of Aquinas, Bellarmine, and Suarez will often be a matter of hearsay, not

100

of first-hand acquaintance; still, they are in full revolt against their own theological formation, and for that reason they seem to view any thing new as good. It is important to keep alive in these candidates for graduate degrees a sense of the history of Western theology, because they among graduate students are uniquely acquainted with it, if only by hearsay. The difficulty is that by a certain understandable extension, the matters that are "of Catholic faith" for these students are more numerous than those few but important matters which are indeed of Catholic faith. In the painful process of bringing the data of revelation and dogmatic definition down to size, there are sometimes more casualties of the critical process than the teacher presenting Catholic theology in an intellectually critical spirit intends.

Students in Roman Catholic graduate schools of religion, whether priests or otherwise, tend to spend their first semester in a state of anxiety over what they call the "negative spirit" that attends the courses they are following. In fact, the so-called negativism may be a healthily constructive positivism in intent, and even in the way in which the material is presented. Many students are unable to see any process in operation, however, other than a negation of positions they once held with the certainty of faith. Critical debunkers of falsely held positions are few enough in Roman Catholic graduate schools. Any who profess their specialty in a genuinely critical spirit are likely to be mistaken for deniers of a faith which invites elaboration under the rubric: "theologians hold."

The convention in Roman Catholic theological exploration up until two or three decades ago was the propounding of a thesis, by which was meant a declaration of the faith of the Church or a theological position on that faith. This thesis, which was in possession, could then be argued on the basis of the biblical data and patristic witness, both often fragmentarily proposed, and the theological argument that had been put forward in support of it at some time in the past. Frequently the

101

thesis was proper to neither the high medieval period nor the Tridentine era but to the nineteenth century Roman universities, where the professors were in a much more closed situation than either the Scholastics or the Counter-Reformation figures. This mode of procedure tends to fade rapidly in Roman Catholic seminaries. In its place is put a much more satisfactory exegesis of the biblical, patristic, and later theological texts. Contemporary graduate students in nonclerical Roman Catholic universities tend to wish to proceed immediately from biblical exegesis to the works of contemporary theologians (e.g., Rahner, Schillebeeckx, Congar) without having paid serious or, in fact, any attention to the intervening centuries.

Even though mention of certain of our theological labors in the past describes a world well lost, it is inconsonant with the Roman Catholic view of tradition as an illuminator of the meaning of the biblical Word to omit any historical considerations whatever in the search for the meaning of that Word. Ahistorical theologians are the bane of any Christian communion, but it may be enlightening to readers of this essay to know how difficult it is for Roman Catholic professors of theology to keep this historical sense alive. One virtue of seminary education, as it existed in this country up to Vatican II, was that its graduates had heard an exposition of almost every theological position that was ever current in Roman Catholic circles, no matter how poorly the work of synthesis might have been done. The graduate school teacher could build on a set of learnings which were common to priests and to non-clerical religious whose theological studies were done in the seminary mold. The recent college graduate who is doing graduate studies in religion or theology, however, frequently comes to it without presuppositions. This is either because he simply has not done much college work in the field, or more usually, because such college work as he has had was not marked by many presuppositions. The existential character of much modern Catholic theology is, in other words, a mixed blessing, just as the previous theology of the Roman schools had been. As between mixed blessings, most graduate school teachers would probably opt for the new sort, unless of course it should be accompanied by a shallow arrogance on the part of the students who find themselves in this condition. But in such cases, a sense of historical theology must simply be supplied.

A final consideration in this important matter is the high degree of vulnerability of our Roman Catholic theologians. Here the clerics who hold unpopular views are in worse condition than the laity, even when these happen to be the emerging majority views of Vatican II. There is still nothing resembling full academic freedom in Catholic theological circles except under such an umbrella as the concept "university" can provide. Seminary formation is fated to be timid and basically ineffective to meet the challenge the priesthood poses until the best professors of theology available to seminary students cease to be subject to summary dismissal without a hearing.

9.

FAITH AND
MODERN SUBJECTIVE THOUGHT*

IT IS NOT EASY to delimit the vast field of the theology of faith
with any secure feeling that the choices being made are the right
ones. Let us speak of certain difficulties that many modern men
have in believing, not the ones men have had in the past or, by
some elusive standard of theology textbooks, should be having
in the present.

That means that an extended discussion of the signification of
the New Testament *pístis* and *pisteúein* and their correspondence
to *aman, he"ᵉmīn* and *"ᵉmūnā* will probably serve no useful purpose at this late date. We have available to us the studies of A.
von Schlatter,[1] A. Weiser and R. Bultmann,[2] and more recently
J. Barr.[3] It is universally acknowledged that the notion of
absolute confidence or trust in Yahweh who would surely save
was paramount in the Israelite understanding, the truthfulness
of his word being a less developed but important part of this
utter fidelity. The single Greek noun and verb that did duty for
faith in all its nuances (plus *pistós, oligópistos, pisteúein 'epí,
'ei, 'en*) came to be extended in the New Testament period to
assent to the truth of the gospel ("Repent and believe the good

* From the CTSA Proceedings, June 24–27, 1963.

[1] *Der Glaube in Neuen Testament*, Stuttgart, 1927.

[2] *Theologisches Wörterbuch zum Neuen Testament* IV, Stuttgart, 1959,
pp. 174–230; ET *Faith*, London, 1961.

[3] *The Semantics of Biblical Language*, London, 1961. Cf. esp. Ch. VII,
"On Faith and Truth."

tidings," Jesus in Mk. 1, 15); to acceptance of Christ's word (*rêma*) through hearing (Rom. 10, 18); and to that total disposition of self with regard to Jesus, the faith that gives life (Jn. 3, 15f. and *passim*). In other words, there is no diminution in the New Testament of the Old Testament idea of faith as trust, confidence, commitment of self into God's hands, certitude that God will act to save, or that Christ will "save" in the sense of cure, and all that this may stand for besides; there is at the same time in the New Testament an extension of the idea, whereby it includes accepting as true what is unseen because God himself has provided trustworthy witnesses to it.

It is quite true, in this sense, that there are two types of faith, to use Buber's phrase: trust in God and belief in a true teaching about him and his saving deeds.[4] It is not true to say, as Buber does, that the former, *emūnā*, is the sole type of faith known to Israel as a believing community, and that *pistis* represents the incursion of a Hellenist idea into late Judaism, namely assent by individuals to the truth of propositions that on the face of them are absurd, even contradictory to the biblical or Jewish mentality. These two types of faith are not mutually exclusive but are two sides of the same coin. Better still, there is faith taken generically—confidence, trust in God—one aspect of which, belief in the truth of God's word, comes into focus as a special type of the exercise of that trust.

I do not feel competent to discuss the theories on the psychology of the act of faith presented so completely by R. Aubert in his *Le Problème de l'acte de foi: données traditionelles et résultats des controverses récentes*. Other insights are given by Henri Bars in *The Assent of Faith* and Ignace Lepp in *Atheism in Our Time*.

Still a third idea that needs to be noticed in order to be set aside is the fear that modern Catholic theological writing may be reintroducing the fiduciary faith of the reformers which had

[4] Cf. his *Two Types of Faith*, London and New York, 1952.

as its essence an exclusively volitional or conative emphasis. This simply is not true. Any desire of the Christian to trust God completely when He acts as personal Savior through the blood of His Son on the cross can only please Him. What the Catholics found the reformers guilty of was something quite different, namely, trusting in God as Savior on terms He had not promised. Even a theologian like Aquinas, who so largely defined faith in terms of knowledge ("it is proper to the believer to think with assent," *S. Th.*, II^a II^{ae}, 2,1;4,1) posited the necessity of the command of the will if there is to be faith, since the evidence is insufficient to bring acquiescence. "Faith is a habit of mind whereby eternal life is begun in us making the intellect assent to what is non-apparent." (*Ibid.*, 4,1)

"This act proceeds from the will and the intellect, both of which have a natural aptitude to be perfected in this way. . . . To believe is immediately an act of the intellect, because the object of that act is the *true*, which properly pertains to the intellect" (*Ibid.*, 4,2). Aquinas' distinction with respect to believing that there is a God (material object of faith), believing God the First Truth when He speaks (formal object of faith), and believing *in* God, namely trusting Him by an act of will which moves the intellect to accept all that He reveals to us, is clear and unequivocal. (*S. Th.*, II^a II^{ae}, 2,2) As Canon Mouroux has demonstrated in his modest but impressive study, *I Believe. The Personal Structure of Faith*, the vocabulary of engagement, commitment, and personal encounter that is coming into common use among Catholic writers is to be found in germ in St. Thomas' total treatment of faith.

Faith is what "gives substance to our hopes," the author of Hebrews wrote, "and makes us certain of realities we do not see." (Heb. 11, 1) Now the *hypóstasis* he speaks of, or underlying actuality corresponding to our expectations, the *eléngchos* (*argumentum*) or proof for the unseen has, as we have indicated, God

106

as revealer for its formal object and God himself and all He does for us as material object.

The root difficulty for modern man in New Testament terms is that increasingly he cannot be made to care about realities he does not see. He does not have faith because of all that he has sight of. He tends to say with Laplace in the apocryphal tale, speaking of God: "I have no need of that hypothesis."

The primitives and the ancients needed explanations of natural phenomena largely because so many of these forces were hostile to them, but in any case because they could not readily interpret them. Less and less is man enveloped by this ignorance. He still is not immortal, but he is on the trail of every other secret of the universe. He has less and less to believe because he knows more and more with *scientia*. But does not his mortality through which he will lose all that he knows and has, impress on him the need for faith? It seems that, by and large, his thorough conditioning to a phenomenological world has killed in him all curiosity concerning a world of any other kind. Normally he does not have to seek a blessed release as a means to improved existence. (I speak of modern technological man.) He wants more and better of what he already has, that is all. An immortal life fills him with a faint disgust as too much of a good thing.

What is to be said of the gnawing unhappiness that accompanies much of contemporary man's satisfactions in work and play and acquisition? He tends to feel he can overcome this unhappiness: another job, another woman, another "deal." He'll get by. He is not without his lively hope with respect to worldly benefits that lie in future.

Hedonism, mitigated or total, which philosophically viewed is satisfaction with a closed system of contingent realities, is one danger to faith. The other is magic, that is, the attempt to manipulate natural forces or the will of the gods through signs and talismans. It is a cheap and easy substitute for faith, and it normally wears a religious mask. Simon Magus and the modern faith-healer or purgatorial-society peddler have been with the Church from the beginning. The trappings of religion are always potentially inimical to faith.

Those who profess religion, the "churched" and especially the clergy, need to be men of faith above all. They must flee any tidy arrangements with God which attempt to subordinate his infinite will to theirs. If there is one thing sure about faith it is that it begins and ends with the submission of the human will to the sovereign will of God. The substitution of religious forms and institutions for the faith of Abraham or Mary of Nazareth is presumably what men like Dietrich Bonhoeffer and J. Langmead Casserley, and at another level Tillich, are deploring when they speak of "religion" as the great threat to Christianity. Basically, they mean by religion the sum total of man's quest for God, and by Christianity or faith, God's initiation and continued pursuit of man to endow him with liberty, i.e., the fullness of creaturehood. Karl Barth says: "Religion is unbelief . . . it is concern, indeed we must say it is the one great concern, of godless man."[5]

Theologians such as Daniélou and de Lubac,[6] in their analysis of the appeal of atheist humanism, are prone to say that modern man lacks faith because he actively resists the claims of another who is *totaliter aliter,* but by analogy person and free like himself. God must die if I am to be free, says Sartre. In every exercise of my liberty I create myself anew. If there were a God he would be master and I would be slave; therefore he must die, for I mean to live. From Nietzsche onward men have experienced a kind of jealousy of God. The tragic hero absolutely requires to be tragic, to be unfulfilled, as in the novels of André Malraux. If he were happy he would owe his happiness to an-

[5] *Church Dogmatics,* I, 2, New York, 1955, 199f.; cf. J. Langmead Casserley, *The Retreat from Christianity in the Modern World,* London, 1952, pp. 42–68.

[6] Cf. J. Daniélou, *The Scandal of Truth,* Baltimore, 1962; H. de Lubac, *The Drama of Atheist Humanism,* London, 1949.

other, a thought he cannot abide. His wretchedness at least is his own—the sign that he is beholden to no one.

We have in the subjective stream of thought of the last one hundred years both the supreme threat to true faith and its potential renewal on better terms than ever before. Faith has no automatic element for the Christian. It is an intensely personal act and it is free. At base it is the Infinite knowing himself in us, for there is no *adequatio* between the finite knower and the Infinite known. God must enter into us, become the ground or fundament of our mind and will, if we are to know him in any true sense. Our "faith is not built on human wisdom but on the power of God." (1 Cor. 2, 5). Is this work of God in us which we call faith destructive of human autonomy or liberty? It is destructive of neither. It is the working together of a creature, whose highest attribute is that he is free, with the supremely Free, ensuring not the enslavement of the creature but his fullest liberty.

For all who are moved by the Spirit of God are sons of God. The spirit you have received is not a spirit of slavery, leading you back into a life of fear, but a Spirit that makes us sons, enabling us to cry, 'Abba! Father!' (Rom. 8, 14ff.)

In this conception of the liberty of faith, the word "submission" must be understood correctly. The Christian in faith submits himself freely to the Infinite whom he cannot comprehend. This inevitably gives the appearance of a loss of freedom because man cannot in fact foresee exactly where this submission will lead him. He is no longer consciously master of himself in knowing Another whom he knows *not* more than he knows. He must trust that this Other wills his own good more than he himself knows how to will it. Our being as freedom-for-God becomes vocal (Rom. 8, 14ff.), and we as sons, not slaves, respond with this being of ours to God as Father. God is both the object and the end of faith, in scholastic terminology; "end" in the sense of the highest good of man to be achieved, once known, through an act of will.

Modern man has been conditioned to see his own liberty as his highest characteristic.[7] He can only come to faith if he sees in God someone who, above all, stands ready to promote his liberty and not negate it.

The roots of modern subjectivity are found in Schleiermacher who taught that God transcends both nature and spirit but is found in religious feeling. Kantian philosophy with its autonomous ego, its preeminence of the subject, and the Hegelian variant on it, brought on this response of men like Schleiermacher, who meant to be Christian and was at least religious, and Kierkegaard, who *was* Christian in the realm of deepest sentiment. Both rejected the compact "system" of Hegel which had an answer for everything in heaven and on earth; even though Kierkegaard found Schleiermacher wanting, he is not far separated from him religiously. Schleiermacher posited the transcendent, the beyond ("Religion is the intuition of the infinite, the feeling of absolute dependence"), while Kierkegaard declared that man was to be saved by his passion for the Infinite—the form his concern for ultimacy might take once he had been faced with the scandal of the cross. There is undoubtedly an object for Kierkegaard, and it is the paradox of a God-man who died for us. His famous dictum (1846) was: "The passion of the infinite is precisely subjectivity and thus subjectivity becomes the truth."[8] Subjective thinking is infinitely absorbed thinking; man's task is to "become a subject," to re-create himself over and over

---

[7] "[For] medieval man . . . the real was what is, was, and has always been. I might say with regard to modern man that for him the real is what is yet to be, what will come into being through him, through man. . . . For modern man *progress* is *the* reality. And history for him is this progress. God always serves man in history, no matter how man may conceive it. If contemporary history has a greater forward dimension than backward, we who are custodians of faith must know this." Friedrich Gogarten, *The Reality of Faith*, Philadelphia, 1959, p. 53.

[8] *Concluding Unscientific Postscript*, Princeton, 1941, p. 181.

again, to bring the truth to pass *in him* as a quality of his own being or existence.

Friedrich Gogarten says that faith will save man only after he has come to reflect on his thoroughgoing impotence before God: from God he has his entire being (1 Cor. 4, 7), which is not integrated into the cosmos as part of it but is called by God as a whole self over against the cosmos and which will not achieve authentic selfhood until man sees himself as one who has no other being than the *being in responsibility* to which the call of God calls him.[9] From the standpoint of faith he may not avoid this responsibility. He must be himself before God. This work, of course, unlike other works, he cannot complete by his own power.

"Adapt yourselves no longer to the pattern of this present world, but let your minds be remade and your whole nature thus transformed." (Rom. 12, 2) This advice of Paul to the Romans is capable of fulfillment through the gift that God in his grace has given; though we work out our salvation it is a suffering, a *páthos,* something that happens to us and in us: "It is God who works in you, inspiring both the will and the deed, for his own chosen purpose." (Phil. 2, 13)

There are familiar echoes in Gogarten's statement, not so much Lutheran—except for the implied duality of man and world—but, in his "authentic selfhood," of Heidegger's authentic existence (*eigentlich Dasein*). Gogarten's "being in responsibility" has resonances in any number of concepts ranging from Heidegger's "resolvedness" (*Entschlossenheit*) to the "decision" (*Entscheidung*) of Bultmann, the "choice of the *Pour-soi*" of Sartre, the "creativity" or growth toward open community of Marcel, and the state of "ultimate concern" of Tillich. We shall not stop to examine the complex thought edifices of these men, even supposing we could do so adequately. It should suffice to list some of the characteristics of modern subjectivity as ex-

[9] Gogarten, *op. cit.,* pp. 37f.

pressed by them, whether its metaphysical presuppositions are atheist, agnostic, Jewish, or Christian, to see what elements in it can contribute to the profession of Catholic faith.

First of all, there is its concern with the openness of person to person or person to thing, whether this be described as mutuality, the I-Thou relation, intersubjectivity, or love responding to the divine condescension. The position is taken here that man cannot know himself as a person, much less be a person, except he do so through admitting others to a lived relation with himself. If he is merely an essence and knows essences or deals with men and things as objects, using them for his enjoyment, if he confronts realities set over against him or believes teachings, he has not made the first step toward realizing himself. His task is to make himself, to come to be, and no affirmation that he ontologically *is* and the world *is* or God *is* has any meaning until he begins to give himself and to admit others so as to find himself.

Second, there is the idea of investing experienced phenomena with value, or holding that nothing has meaning unless by an act of will I declare that it has meaning for me. For Kierkegaard this means coming to terms with—admitting into our lives—an Object, which is God's deed to save us in Christ. For Sartre it is imposing meaning or value on brute fact (*En-soi*), any meaning we choose to give it so long as we take the responsibility for the act of choice. I cut down my aged parent with an axe; it is a bloody and repulsive deed, but it is my deed. I am other and more than I was before doing it. Though they guillotine me for it I shall go to my absurd and inevitable death a little less nauseous, less vertiginous, than I was before I stood on the brink of the abyss of my possible free choices, for at least I had the courage to reduce them by one.

Note in all this two things: that my liberty is the supreme good, and that neither Kierkegaard's nor Sartre's system (if Kierkegaard will forgive me the term) is to be thought of as an immanentism. This is an important observation, especially as regards Kierkegaard. "Subjectivity becomes the truth" for him in the sense that nothing is true for the subject, least of all Christianity, until he appropriates it, that is, takes in by faith the Christian message of life and salvation which God reveals. There is no truth until I have made it my truth.

Similarly, neither Sartre, Marcel, nor any of the others is an immanentist as Socrates was, in whom all truth lay in a fetal state, to be made his conscious possession maieutically. All modern subjective thinkers posit a real world of fact "out there." Their point is that it stays "out there" until subjectivity comes along to relieve it of its meaninglessness as mere object. Now all this bears some relation to the part of the will in the act of divine faith, by which a man chooses to participate in the life of God once the intellect has identified it as a good for him. He comes to belief because he knows something of God and salvation, and in willing to believe he comes to know God even further as *his* good.

Third and last, it takes courage (Tillich), a leap (Kierkegaard), evangelical decision (Barth), a revolt (Camus) to lay hold either of the paradox of God's love or the liberty that delivers one from absurdity, until that last and fatal absurdity, death, closes in. Kierkegaard and Barth express themselves as Christians here by saying that only the Holy Spirit can achieve in us the transition from being faced by the gospel or by other Christian witness, "evidences" as we call them to faith. The data do not exact faith. They may even point in the opposite direction. What we stress here is that besides (1) an openness to others and (2) a dominance of the subject, there is for modern subjectivity (3) a motivating force in man which acts to achieve in him his self-realization, or salvation, or freedom. These are some characteristics of contemporary thought patterns often lumped together as existential because of a concern for the concrete man who is, in his response to his life situation.

113

Let us conclude by confining ourselves to the faith situation of those Roman Catholics whom we serve in our ministry as theologians, priestly or other. What is their condition vis-à-vis the modern spirit? How are they affected by contemporary challenges to faith?

First, I would say, their faith is considerably weakened by the widespread failure of the Catholic community to commit itself to human liberty as a great Christian good. This is especially true in seminaries. We are not raising up great men of faith, among other reasons because we do not consult each other's freedom as God consults ours. This makes it nearly impossible for seminary students to gain an adequate idea of who God is. They will not commit their destinies to Him fully and freely unless they have some splendid analogues of trust and trustworthiness and truth in their human brothers. The same is true of the parishioners, college students, and others whom the priest —man of faith *kat'exoken*—serves.

Second, since the man in grace is the highest work of God in all visible creation, he in whom the Spirit dwells is not only the chief external motive for faith but, in our day, rapidly becomes the only motive. Confrontation with the gospel incarnate in a man will achieve what cannot otherwise be achieved, since avenue after avenue effective in other times and cultures is being sealed off. Increased technology is undoubtedly dimming metaphysical concern except in a small group of scientists— the great minority—whose new insight into approximation and indeterminacy in nature is robbing them of false certainties and putting them in search of an ontological ground for the teleology cum flux which they observe. Linguistic and logical analysis has all but terminated metaphysical concern among professional philosophers.

Third, there must be on the part of believers full and conscious accord with all progress in the control of the phenomenal world through empirical and social science. Unless *scientia* is given free play, its possible confusions with *fides,* which are manifold, cannot be reduced to the zero point; but they must be, if faith is to be a live option for modern man.

Fourth and last, since man must be confronted with the saving deed of God in his life here and now if he is to have faith—setting aside completely the doubts cast on sacred history in our time as a true record of any such deed in Jesus Christ—the man who is prepared for new faith or growth in faith by the experience of charity must be confronted frequently by God as his Savior. The Church does this in one symbolic way that typifies all the others: she proclaims the Gospel in the context of sacraments celebrated, chiefly the Eucharist, which are the work of our salvation accomplished now. This is, or can be, a genuine confrontation. Some kind of immediate response is required. It is an *experience* of God as Savior. That is why I think we need to name as a major, if not the chief, reason for weakness of faith in Catholic life, whether in parish or college or seminary, the low estate of sacramental celebration and of proclamation of the gospel in all its strength at its center. I mean, quite clearly, that the way we celebrate the liturgy, or more often do not celebrate it, is the key not to all but to much in the modern man's search for faith. Celebration of liturgy to me means regular discussion, in evangelical terms, of the great social and personal problems of our time.

Our faith is weak because we mistrust the great signs of Christ, and conversely our signs are pallid because there is so little faith for them to express.

10.

TRINITARIAN FAITH AND SPIRITUAL LIFE*

THERE IS NO SUCH THING in the Church, we may say, as devotion to the Holy Trinity. There are only Christians who hope to be devout in the presence of their God, who in progressively revealing Himself has invited us to have a part eternally in His inner life.

But the beginning of eternity is now. Grace is the seed of glory. From our baptism we have had the call to a personal relation with each of the three who are the great God transcendently one. We are signed in the seal of the three. Their imprint is irrevocably upon us. We speak of being "configured unto Christ" as sons of the Father in the Holy Spirit. A myriad of analogies has been devised in attempts to capture the reality of the indwelling of the three in the Christian soul. None of them quite succeeds but each is serviceable in its own way, if it is in accord with the ancient faith as the New Testament, the Fathers of the Church, and the Councils bring it to us. Perhaps a better way to express it than to say that the three are in us (since properly speaking God is in relation to no creature, but all are in relation to Him), is to say that we the baptized are in Him in a sense more intimate than any creature may be said to be in Him, that is, *toward* or *unto* Him in virtue of His invitation and our acceptance, which is already a movement Godward.

Our Christian life is nothing if it is not a trinitarian life. This does not mean a static condition of relation to a static three,

* First published in *Bible, Life, and Worship*, The Liturgical Conference, Washington, D.C., 1962, pp. 125–128.

even by way of fullest commitment. No, there is first of all the inward and eternal dynamic of the godhead, which finds expression in an outgoing action of self-revelation by the three. Their interrelation is one of love, and the love overflows. It takes the form of invitation to the special and intimate sonship of God we have spoken of. Our brotherhood in humanity with one who is eternally a Son is our title, so to say, to consideration. God is forever being Father to His Son, and the Son stands eternally in a relation of sonship to His Father. And He who is eternally Son became Brother to us.

There never was a "when-this-was-not," we say of the Father-Son relation, in a barely successful attempt to keep all considerations of time out of a matter that transcends time utterly. But this twofold relation of fatherhood and sonship is not the only active-passive intercommunion among those who are One in God. There is the eternal going-forth of a third, whom the sacred sources—chiefly the New Testament—never fail to describe in terms of a holy counsel rooted in love. The interaction of Father and Son is not fruitless. It terminates in a Person whom the two commonly "breathe forth." The Scriptures are thrown back desperately on figure-language here: *ru'ach, pneûma* (*Spiritus, Geist, Ghost*),—they all mean breath or wind, a great, effective reality quite unseen. The common production by Father and Son of a third is called by theology a work of "active spiration." The Spirit thus breathed forth stands in a relation to the two from whom He eternally comes (or proceeds) as one who has His divine being from them: the relation of "passive spiration," in theological language.

The terms of theology need not detain us, but the reality of the Christian revelation must. If we grasp the chief notion Jesus came to share, namely that God is a Father to us in a new and unheard of way; if we come to learn the sublimity of His own mediatory office with respect to us His brothers; if we learn there is no holiness for man except that the All-holy should

117

sanctify him, then we have taken in three basic truths of Christian faith. We must make one truth of them, however, just as we must reconcile in some fashion in our intellects the overmastering truth that the three are yet One.

The first disciples, in preaching Jesus as bearer of that Name by which alone men are saved, began by underlining the ancient belief of Israel that the Lord is majestically and incomprehensibly One. He, *Yahweh Sebaoth,* is the God whose proper name is Lord; besides Him there is no other. Yet there is another who has been constituted by this God (*Theós*) Lord and Christ *Kýrios kai Chrístos.* A Servant has been raised up to glory by God as a reward of His obedience unto death. He is at the right hand of God the Father (*Theós*) and He shares the inexpressible glory of that God as a thing earned—therefore by right. Note that the New Testament attributes such glory to Jesus the Man of Nazareth, in the Acts of the Apostles especially; in other places, particularly the fourth gospel, it is clearly stated that the only Son shared in His Father's glory from the beginning, therefore as eternal Son but not as Son enfleshed.

Without confusion or strain the first Christians took in as part of the message preached, then written, the fact of these two who do nothing to destroy the oneness of God. The Lord of Israel was indeed more fully one than before, if we may so speak, in that, so rich is He in His being, He is now known to have an image, a splendor, a refulgence of Himself. Nor is the unity of God lessened, rather enhanced when it is seen that the treasure of possessing a knowledge of this relation of Father and Son has been shared with the believer through the action of yet a third who is *Paráklētos, Advocatus.* He has been sent for the work of comforting and supporting men in the absence of Jesus, who had fulfilled that office during His earthly stay.

The first Christians, in other words, took in the mysterious fact of the three, which has nothing to do with the number three. The term is an analogue, an approximation taken out of

118

our human experience to instruct us on matters we have little experience of, just as the words "Father" and "Son" are facts of our lives that will communicate the relationships in God best, though the relations in God are separated from human fatherhood and sonship by an infinity. The unique element of Christian faith with respect to its preaching about God was the distinctness of the three. This conception did nothing to weaken the concept of His unity or uniqueness.

He was known through what He had done for us, though He was as He is before ever He *had* done for us. The Christian idea of God is of One active to save us. Israel's idea had not been different. She too had known Him in His saving work. But as His salvation of us grew richer, so our knowledge of the One who saved us grew richer.

You know, I assume, what happened during the Arian threat, how the trinitarian mystery lost its contour, so to say, when the fully divine status of the Son was denied by the followers of Arius, and affirmed in response by the Catholics. The subsequent denial by the Macedonian heretics of the Spirit's full godhead brought a Catholic response equally resounding. It was now, "Glory be to the Father *and* to the Son *and* to the Holy Spirit" instead of, "*through* the Son *in* the Holy Spirit." Catholic faith in Christ's divinity was maintained, gloriously maintained, but at the price of silencing us on the precise way in which God saves us, in our very attempts to glorify Him for having saved us.

We suffer these handicaps still.

The preface of the Trinity in the Roman rite, which was developed in the middle ages but officially adopted for Sunday use only in 1759, reflects this state of affairs. Like the Athanasian Creed, as it is called, this preface puts all its emphasis on the coequal status of the Persons; there is none on how they redeemed us. In this, the opening prayer of the canon of the Roman Mass is quite unlike the conclusion: "Through Him and with

119

Him and in Him, in the unity of the Holy Spirit, all honor and glory are yours, Almighty Father, forever and ever. Amen."

The remedy of this situation regarding the divine Trinity in Western piety lies chiefly in a restoration of Christ's mediatory role. There must be no fear on our part of being taken for Arians by those who have forgotten the correct and Catholic emphasis on the mutual relations of the three, as we know them from the revelation of the redemptive mystery. The Christian is in a unique relation to the Son because of his common manhood with Him. Sons of God we had somehow been as creatures; now we are brothers to the only Son. This puts us in a new relation not only to the Word, our Brother, but to the Father and Spirit, in company of whom He possesses the fullness of deity, and to each of whom He is uniquely related.

We pray to Christ, yes, addressing Him with complete attention to His role with respect to us. This means we pray through Him to the Father in the Holy Spirit. We adore Him because He is the eternal Word, but if we adore Him only and do not beg Him to exercise His mediatory office with the Father for us, we disregard the incarnation through which we know both Him and the Father.

We are brothers to the Son, sons to the Father, formed as a community of sons by the Love who binds the two together. This Spirit is the bond of unity in the Church, just as He is the end-term of all divine interaction. He is the outer limit of the divine dynamic, and the form or limit of the community of charity which we are. Of Mary, the perfect type of the Christian, we say that she is offspring of the Father, mother of the Son, and spouse of the Spirit. No one of us has the same role as she in the mystery of salvation. All of us, however, are called to a distinct, personal relation with each of the eternal three.

11.

How Worldly Must the Church Be?*

THE QUESTION, "How worldly must the Church be?" puts one in mind of the reply of the contemporary British philosopher who was asked whether he thought life was worth while. He said, after a pause, "It depends on what you mean by while."

What do you mean by "worldly," not to speak of "world"? What do you mean by "Church"? How exigent is your "must," how qualitative your "how"?

The question of the Church's worldliness is not a new question, but one newly and importantly raised by contemporary theologians of secularity. When the popes made boyhood cardinals of their illegitimate sons, when Wolsey built Hampton Court and the Archbishop of Salzburg a rural retreat for his mistress, when Church and state make common cause against the Jew, or Church and mammon against the worker, we at least know where we stand. This is the Church grown worldly in the sense of bowing to Rimmon, whoring after the idol of gold or lechery or self-preservation or power. It is a clear disregard of the injunction of James to keep onself "unspotted by this world," understood to mean all perversion of the right use of things in a way which is set against God because inimical to man.

Do believers, Jewish or Christian, hold large properties individually or corporately? This could be worldly in the sense

* First published in *Worship in the City of Man,* The Liturgical Conference, Washington, D.C., 1966, pp. 49–56.

repudiated by the gospel. It could also be an exercise of wisdom of the kind Jesus and the rabbis of Judaism enjoined.

Does Monsignor Mushmouth use Old Spice, does Sister Marilyn wear mesh stockings? You may fault their taste, but they are happily and dumbly innocent of the gospel charge of worldliness. Their cosmos may be painfully bourgeois, but it is in no sense the *kósmos*—the "world"—of the Johannine writings, which is set against God and his love. At one time in Christian history worldliness may have meant a congeries of little conceits, petty vanities, but that is a paltry use of the term and one well beneath our notice. If the term "worldly" is to be pejorative at all, it should be used grandly—namely, to describe that demonic element in human life that challenges the divine, Beelzebul in the place of Jesus, anti-God dethroning God, but piously and in God's name.

The "worldly" so conceived is whatever is inimical to the freely chosen service of our heavenly Father. Against this conception of the worldly the Church must struggle until the end of time. As a holy community the Church knows it can never exorcise the demonic utterly, either from humanity or from itself, but it also realizes that it may never relax vigilance. The world in this sense finds expression everywhere: in armies, in commerce and industry, in the arts, in the organizing of lust, but especially and most tellingly within the Church itself. There the "world" of arrogance before God is a perpetual Trojan horse. The world present in the bosom of the Church means that that portion of the true Church which exists outside the visible Church will always be able to be stigmatized by members of the visible Church as "the world." The supreme blasphemy for Christians consists in repudiating the spirit of Christ as it is found apart from their midst, the prince of this world being so firmly entrenched in their midst. In that sense—and not so much in the sense of Alexander VI and his concubines, poor Wolsey and his toys—the Church must have a care for worldliness through all her days: blessing military machines, fearing intellect, dividing humanity into "we" and "they," putting trust in the sufficiency of self.

The opposition between Church and world is popularly conceived, however, on other terms than those of this unmistakable New Testament antithesis. There is a mistakable New Testament opposition between Church and world, and since apostolic times we have been making that mistake. Let us examine how it came to be, and see what we can begin to do about correcting the error.

To begin at the beginning: the world and all that is in it is good. From whenever it first came to be, this has been so. But men did not know this from the beginning. For eons they lived in fear of baleful spirits in rocks and trees, of crocodiles in rivers, which ate their children. There was deity in the river, deity in the sun and moon, and at a late date in human history, deity in grain and wine. "Everything is full of gods" was the conviction of the relatively late and sophisticated Greek philosopher Thales. For Israel, likewise a latecomer on the human scene, nothing on earth was full of gods. This people stripped the pantheon of the cosmos bare. Yahweh dwelt beyond the heavens and there alone. The earth was the home of fish and birds and beasts, and of their master, man. Yahweh was intimately present to this world, the work of His hands. In His power He was closer to man than man was to himself, but He was as distinct from man and the rest of creation as the heavens were high above the earth. The myth or poem of a universe full of gods was a myth that Israel could not sing. Because Yahweh was her teacher, this people learned from Him to demythologize the universe. Israel took it from the hands of the high gods of her neighbors, Baal and Ashera, Moloch and Chamos—all the major and minor nature deities—and gave it back to man. "The earth is Yahweh's," her poets sang. He has made man supreme over it, constituted him "a little less than the angels." The world

123

is the place where man lives and works and fights his battles, with Yahweh as Israel's champion. Space or place on earth is one dimension of man's life, time or history is the other. God the unseen, God the holy, God who was there when the foundations of the hills were laid and who will be there when the heavens have worn out like a garment, God is the meaning of man's life on the earth. He is the one, indispensable point of reference, the personal and free condition of man's personal and free existence.

For the men of the Bible wine was good, though drunkenness was an evil. Sex was good, though lechery was an evil. Food was good; so were a man's flocks, his herds, his home, his children's children gathered around his table. A man could sin through greed, through murder, through cruelty to slaves. His greatest sin, however, was described in the Bible as folly: the blasphemy of saying, "There is no God." Since palpably God was, this could only mean: "I shall live as if he were not. What I have, I have of my own cunning and skill." Or in today's idiom: "I'll go it alone."

Biblical man was a thoroughgoing worldling, but one no aspect of whose life was lived without reference to Yahweh the holy.

With the person and work of Jesus there came a difference, from the point of view of those who believed in Him. He was thought by them to have inaugurated a new era in human history, a fresh eon. In His own person, under Yahweh whom He called His Father, He comprised something new for humanity. The great seal of the United States has on its obverse the legend in Latin, "A new order of history." The thought, of course, is biblical. It meant for the Jew any great turning point, but notably that toward the last age of earth. It meant for the Jew and the Greek who believed in Jesus the last times, the final eon, at the center of which was Jesus, made Lord and Messiah.

And here we have a problem.

124

For Jesus lived in a period of history when Israel was caught up in patterns of flight from the realities of history. The mood was "apocalyptic" or "eschatological." The terms may be strangely Greek in sound but the ideas are familiar enough. Hope was lodged in the imminent end of the world. Soon there should come a thousand years of peace and plenty, Israel's feet on the necks of her enemies by the power of her avenging Lord. In this vain dreaming, signs of the wrath to come were looked for in the sun and moon and stars.

There was, moreover, in Jesus' day, a second stream of thought abroad in Israel. It was Zoroastrian in origin, though it was to be found everywhere in the ancient world: the mutual opposition of light and darkness, spirit and matter, good and evil, the unseen world of enduring reality and this world of appearance and illusion.

I said we have a problem here. The problem is this. Was Jesus, were his followers the captives of this late-Jewish mentality, or was this Son of Man quite free of the confusions of Jewish sectarians like the men of the Dead Sea community? Was our Lord solidly with Moses and the prophets in having God and the world straight, while his followers from the beginning came to misconstrue in some measure his reading of creation? We know this much from the New Testament writings: the authors, all of them Jewish in outlook, were so convinced that Jesus was God's answer to man's existential anguish—to sin and pain and death—that they stressed the world as a place of evil and demonic power. They were not Platonic philosophers regretting this world as a world of appearances. They did not forget their ancient Jewish convictions about the goodness of the earth, man's home. But their great concern was human rebellion or sin, and they put forward God's answer, the obedient Jesus, who had called his followers out of the world, protected them from the world, and sent them into the world to be a living reproach to the world. This, I say, is the prevailing theme of the New Testament.

Decades passed after Jesus' glorification, and with them any false notions the early Christians had had of the imminent dissolution of the universe. What did not pass was the opposition of the Christian community to the works of this world, a matter on which they were not entirely clear. They did not reprobate sex, but they were afraid of it. They did not turn their backs on ownership, but they were somewhat leery of it. Jesus, after all, had taught simplicity of life. He favored *áskēsis*. Prayer, fasting, and almsgiving were high-priority values for him. So was abstention from sex, for those who could take it for the sake of the kingdom. But this approach to life accorded well with that of the Stoic philosophers and of certain Jewish sages affected by non-Jewish thought. Shortly, the Christians were following in the way of a non-biblical piety, at least in part.

When the Christians gained practical freedom in the Constantinian era, they tended to abuse their power. Moreover, excesses of pleasure marked the Christian, as they marked every man. To check himself, he was constantly retreating from this world and claiming gospel sanction for doing so. He went into the Egyptian desert in the third century; in Benedict, that great romantic, he ran away from Rome in the sixth century; he tightened his cincture with Bernard in the twelfth century and the cord around his waist with Francis in the thirteenth century. Both Francis and Dominic sang the praises of creation to a world either wallowing in it or, like the Albigenses, fearful of it, yet they themselves "weren't having any." Creation is good, and in Christ's person it comes to its intended perfection, yet the old enemies, sin and Satan, are still with us, and man does not trust himself sufficiently to enjoy things with a clear conscience. The sad fact is that the world, man's home, can at any moment, by an evil alchemy, become the world set against its Author in sin. The believer in God, Christian or Jew, bears the awful responsibility of esteeming creation to the full, while fearing the power of creation to turn on God in his, man's, own person and going an independent way. The ambiguity of cleaving to this world while at the same time disengaging from it is one that will never disappear for the man of faith, who gleans something of its mystery.

That is a very brief statement of the problem historically. Does it say anything at all about the problem contemporarily?

Well, first of all, the questions modern man asks are not in the same order as those asked in times past. He is no longer in awe of the cosmos as he used to be. Nature holds fewer and fewer secrets for him. He is in a continuing struggle for freedom, even from God if it seems that God is restraining his freedom. He lives in the city increasingly. Its values are his values. He can achieve, he can accomplish, he can move. What he hasn't yet got he hopes to acquire. In any case, he means to hold on to what he has. He has his political ideals, his ideals in health and education, his convictions about a good life for himself and his children. He is not much intimidated by a God who sees his every movement, nor does he fear the "loss of his soul." Death is both mysterious and regrettable but he does not think about it much, nor shrink from it when he does. He is not very curious about it; it is an unknown. Besides there is too much living to do.

In describing modern man I have probably fallen into the trap of all contemporary generalizers, whether they be theologians, sociologists, or essayists for *Time*. I may have constructed a figment. Many modern men are poorly adjusted, to the point of mental illness; millions are simply in a daily struggle for existence; untold numbers live consciously before God, or under the bullying influence of a religious superego. In other words, modern man is terribly various. To homogenize him to our taste may be to obliterate him. If we do that we cannot

127

even put the question of his stance in faith or unfaith, because there is no recognizable person there who is a believer.

I am going to propose a number of values to which I think the Church—understood most broadly as the community that trusts in God—must adhere in today's secular world.

The Church must not fear any human value, any human passion, any human achievement. If it does, it proves that it believes neither in creation nor redemption. Such fears are more likely to constitute a reproach to humanity than a service.

The Church has no need of distinctive dress or behavior to mark off its membership. Love is the way all man shall know us. We need to discover if we really believe that dictum of the Savior.

The Church needs to worry terribly about appearance or show. Men of our time are regularly lied to by propagandists, politicians, and advertisers. They fear being "conned." They know that religious bodies are suing for their attention like other bodies; they assume they are being lied to by them like all the rest. When in fact they are—as is all too often the case—their worst suspicions are confirmed. I did not say that modern man is committed to honesty or authenticity. I said that he suspects the opposite in every case, and that it will be a long, slow pull on the Church's part to convince him that it is otherwise with her.

The Church must stand for human progress, but it need not do so under any specific ecclesial identity or cultic pattern. Indeed, the moment the Christian says, "It is my charity wherewith I love you," or "My Roman Catholic faith prompts me to this," he needs to fear whether he any longer believes or loves. Not only Christians can be anonymous. The Holy Spirit, the world's most authentic person, is the most anonymous of all.

The Church is a community that prays. It does not hesitate to call on God as its Father. In fact, it is under compulsion of love to do so. A Church which is totally secular, in the sense of being committed to the needs of the brother where he is without ever turning to the Father communally in prayer, is not the Church of Christ. The Father with his Son and Spirit is both immanent to us and transcends us. This is not an either/or situation; it never has been such, nor will it ever be. But God is someone whom Jesus tells us to call on as "Abba," Father, by name, in the company of brothers. We need not always do so. We need do so only at certain times—the great minority of moments in life. But we must pray to him, together, at times.

Lastly, the Church needs to choose signs out of man's everyday life that stand for the God who is. These signs will be symbols as well as signs. I mean, they will participate somehow in the reality of Him who alone is holy. But all of creation is in that position of the potential symbolizing of Him who is holy. He first made it, then reestablished it more marvelously still.

Man is the great sign of God's person, his freedom, and his love. Therefore the great symbols will not be fire or water, soil or sky. They will be sex and food and speech and love. They will be the activities of man—his everyday activities in secular life—become the symbols of the Father who is prayed to. All the world is called to be Church, though not all the world *is* Church. All creation, starting with man himself, is the bridge from world to Church and Church to world.

To answer our question, then, "How worldly must the Church be?" we answer: "Thoroughly worldly, while never acquiescing in sin."

12.

The Sister and the Public Worship
of the Church*

WHAT DO I MEAN when I use the word "liturgy"? I mean
your prayer in union with Christ in a way that gives you as
much human satisfaction as this sublime activity can yield. I
mean the greatest possible measure of awareness of doing the
right thing about your personal and corporate relation to God.
I mean bringing to a kind of peak all the ascetical practices you
have ever engaged in, all the strength you have ever derived
from reading the Bible or any spiritual book. I mean your sense of
having met God, experienced Him through the person of Jesus
Christ, in the conjunction of word and sign that constitutes any
sacramental rite.

Liturgy is by no means a reproach or an affront to our religious sensibilities. It is, above all, a sign, a natural, easy sign of
the love for Christ and in Christ which we experience inwardly.
It is not a Procrustean bed on which we are stretched by a host
who knows what is good for us, who lops off an arm here and
a leg there, and says, "Now you'll fit, and because you fit you'll
be happy."

No, liturgy goes in quite another direction. It says, "Have
you had salvation proclaimed to you?" You answer, "Yes, from
my earliest youth."

"You know, then, how Jesus died for our sins, and was raised

* From the *Proceedings of the Institute on Problems That Unite Us*,
Sisters of Charity, B.V.M., Dubuque, 1966.

up in glory from the dead, so that we too might live with him?"

"From my earliest recollection," you say, "I have never had any other gospel preached to me. It is the faith in which I live, and in which I mean to die."

So far so good. Now liturgy's problem is quite simply to give the best expression possible to that faith which you already hold. We must not for a moment think of the liturgy in terms of an arrangement external to ourselves. It is not something "out there," something we are expected to do and do correctly. Even the phrase "summit and source of the Church's activity" can be deceptive. A summit is a high peak which is there to be scaled. A source is a reservoir or font, that which alone provides. Do you see what I've done? I've interpreted the liturgy in terms of a barrier, a challenge, something that builds in its own resistance because you're told how good it is for you, how necessary, how indispensable.

The liturgy is what you ought to want to do when you've just pulled a low trick on a friend and are sorry; when you've put in a frustrating day and are defeated; when you've been up three or four hours and are happy, or a half hour and are groggy; when you've lost your best friend in death and are grieving; when you want to rejoice in seeing your sister taken as a bride. Whenever, in a word, you wish to take strength from the breathtaking fact that Christ died for our sins and was raised up for our justification, there is this sacred behavior waiting to be engaged in, which will help that mystery become a reality in your life.

I should be pleased if you thought freely and easily about the liturgy, not regretfully or resentfully, or even with propriety. Think, for a moment, of how you might be happiest if left to yourself in planning this joint enterprise of prayer. Some song, great melodies you feel strongly attracted to, even though you can't sing them very well. Some stately movement which is at the same time comfortable and easy, not stiff or contrived. Some

131

Bible reading, familiar enough that you're not put off by it but mysterious enough that you hear a new thing each time a passage is read to you. Some prayers which speak great sentiments of praise and gratitude, not: "Take them, place them in your open, broken Sacred Heart," or some similar unmanageable proposal. Some time for quiet reflection, genuine contemplation, built into the rite. Enough of the familiar, the expected, so as not to make you feel a stranger in a strange place. Enough of the new, the freshly experienced, that you are not threatened with tedium in a great and sacred event which, of its nature, recurs. And lastly, a human happening characterized by love which really shows forth the reality of Christ in bread or flowing water or wine or upraised healing hand or oil.

Christ left us certain signs of faith to express our faith. He and His early followers knew the reality of love.

They had a washing and an unguent and a meal and a reconciling or supplicating word to manifest this love. They did simple, easy things, things that were part of them, that came out of their human experience, and they called this sacred behavior *liturgy*. Is there a volume of choreography for the rain dance of the Zuñi Indians? What has happened to the book of stage directions for Ellen Terry when she was Ophelia to Sir Henry Irving's Hamlet? Have you seen the marked copy of Wladislaw Richter's score? In the hands of great artists, the precise *how* and *why* of their art gradually recedes. They are caught up in an action that is exactly right for now. They can express themselves in no other way. Similarly, constitutions and diocesan directories and what you can and cannot do in "this diocese" are not the heart of liturgy. They are working drawings for the uninitiate, the crude sketches and outlines that were first needed for those who meant to perform a great work of art: I mean corporate prayer.

What is the reality in the situation? I am still a slave to the missal, even in its relatively simple and short canon, after twenty-four years, because I was trained that way. When they first turned me around to lead you in prayer I was thoroughly embarrassed. My eye is still glued to the score. But, then, do you sisters know ten, twenty, fifty great hymns by heart—a dozen Masses, a chorale or two? Are you rushing back to the sacristy proposing to me that I modify my practice for the day and celebrate as you do in Winesburg, Ohio; Gibbsville, Pa.; No. Dak., So. Dak., Minn., Wis., and Ia.?

Now these things I'm speaking of are not wild dreams. They are the reality of liturgy. It is personal; it is communal; it is local. It is as much a part of you as the way you walk or speak or dance; it is the one mystery of Christ celebrated through a sevenfold prism and in a myriad of ways.

I am not proposing antinomian behavior: contravention of the Church's law. I am trying to describe liturgy for what it is, so that we will begin to think rightly about it, and act rightly about it. You are Christian women: mature, adult, healthily inhibited, but equally healthily uninhibited. You have sorrows, joys, abilities, possibilities, that are quite special to you individually. You are members of one great community, the human family, and another, the Church. You are at ease, totally adjusted to heaven, to earth, to your enemies, to your friends, when you enter this holy place. There is no place for tension here, the averted gaze, the uncertain ego, the inauthentic self. Here there is a deed to do and a general understanding of how to do it. It is not a nit-picking, particular understanding, specified down to the last detail. That could be death to joy. That could be a sign of servility to the law, and we are here precisely because we are sons and daughters, *filii et filiae*. In this spirit we begin our song, our word, our consecratory prayer, our meal. It is our liturgy; we made it. It came from our minds in faith and our hearts in love. I suppose that up until now I have been speaking of the world of sacramental prayer that *could be*. I should doubtless be speaking of the world of sacramental prayer that more identifiably *is*.

133

All the changes attempted in sacramental celebration up to this point through legislation and pastoral care have as their purpose an increase of the sense of unity among believers. The first effect of the Eucharist, says Aquinas, is the unity of the Church.

In the liturgy there exists a bond which can bring people together, the bond of common language. Love needs common speech; but for centuries in the West we have had some elements of human love without the use of language. The omission has not destroyed love; it has, however, impaired it.

The great concern of the Church is, of course, interiorization of sacred reality. To have speech without communication, to have gesture without meaning, is to threaten the making interior of our possession of divine mystery. It should be obvious that improvement of the outward sign can help achieve a genuine interiority. This does not happen automatically, needless to say. Bad patterns of language, second- or third-rate rhetoric, can become a great distraction; indifferent or sub-standard hymnody will not accomplish the interiority desired. The worshiper is too busy having ruffled feelings over the unsatisfactory sign. I am simply speaking here of the sacramental principle which flows from the mystery of the incarnation. We are body and spirit and we can only be reached through body and spirit. How God gets in touch with angels is something known to him. We know that he reaches psychosomatic man by incorporating truth and beauty in sense and sound. Music in the liturgy is in no sense an independent good. Neither is common song, nor English speech, nor change in posture; none of them is a good taken in itself. Each of these features is meant to be not a distraction from contemplative prayer but an attraction to the very business at hand which is an action, a deed, the reality of which we are invited to contemplate.

One matter crucial here is that the Christian meets God in Jesus Christ primarily in a social situation. The experience of

saving grace comes when two or three, or thousands, come together in Christ's name. When a community is present, however
small, however large, then there is the Church at prayer. We
do not put up with others for practical reasons, in a spirit of
being unable to avoid them. We are spatially located in relation
to other worshipers so that the common action can be best done
by all. That action is a meal.

Only lately in Catholic theological thought are we returning
unanimously to the New Testament idea of the worship of God
through a meal. There had been aberrations in past centuries.
The phenomenon of not receiving the Eucharist was widespread,
so much so that in 1215 A.D. the Church felt that it had to
require people to eat the Lord's body once a year.

John Calvin was on his way to Strasbourg to do some private
study in 1536 when he stopped off on his way to Geneva, there
meeting a man by the name of Edmund Farel. Farel was a
Lutheran, who said that he had worked hard for the last five
years with the people of this city; he asked if the teacher would
please stay. Calvin did stay, and in 1537 he devised a liturgy for
the people. He borrowed it from the reformed community of
Strasbourg. All his time in Geneva over the next two decades
he tried to get this once-Catholic people to celebrate the Lord's
Supper, and by that I mean he tried to get the people to receive
communion, every Sunday. He never succeeded. He got the
reception of the Eucharist up to once a month, but the town
fathers of Geneva and the city's people ultimately defeated him.
They had learned their lesson of a non-Eucharistic life as Catholics all too well.

This describes the end of the medieval period in the
Catholic Church. You have perhaps heard about certain super-
stitious practices which were abroad, such as the desire to see the
host. People used to pay ushers to get them seated in advanta-
geous positions so that they could look at it longest. It became
God's body ("Odds bodkins!" is a corruption of that term).

135

Rather than the flesh of the Son of Man given for the life of the world, which you eat, it became something to gaze upon.

At the theological level it was carefully worked out that the essence of this action was some sort of mystical immolation. It was an offering of Christ to God which, to be effective, didn't need to culminate in an eating except for the celebrant. Even though the implication was that the work of representative sacrifice had been sufficiently achieved by consecration, it was granted that certain important, extra benefits were given to the worshippers who came forward and ate. Such eating comprised a separate matter, in this confused theology of the Mass. The reformers first pleaded with the Roman Church, then scolded her roundly for not insisting on the meal character of the Eucharist. They were quite intransigent against the use of the sacred host in any context other than eating it. We say that they were wrong, that they were heretical in their fulminations against reservation or in calling any use of the Eucharist but nourishment "idolatry"; but in requiring that there be a meal they were not heretical. They were Catholic in that. A false distinction had arisen in Catholic theological consciousness between sacrificial offering and communicating. The reformers were denying that the Mass was a sacrifice, and that hardened the lines. Probably everyone here has been engaged in some slight altercation in the last few years over the question of "making too much out of the Mass as a banquet." Whenever a person says that, you know immediately that he is confused on the nature of the commemorative rite which the Mass is. He is back in the former dispensation. He thinks you have to slaughter a bull or a calf or make Jesus hurt again to have a true sacrifice. He quotes Trent to the effect that the Mass is an unbloody sacrifice, but he wants it bloody or painful somehow, so that it will be a "real and true sacrifice" by his wrong standard. But that is not the faith of the Church. The death of the Lord Jesus, a sorrowful event at the time of its happening, has become a joyous event in its commemoration. He is raised up and brought forth from the tomb, never to die again. At a meal, not otherwise. The Mass for the Catholic is not a sacrifice which has a meal aspect. It is a meal which has a sacrifice aspect. Its very essence is that it is a sacred meal, one in the preparation and consumption of which glory is given to God in the sign of food. The food is the Lord Jesus, whole and entire. He is present sacramentally, not physically, i.e., in the ordinary course of nature. He is present really. We prepare this food so as to eat it, and in eating it we offer to God a sacrifice of praise.

13.

FAITH COMES THROUGH HEARING*

WHEN I WAS in elementary and high school I spent considerable time in the local public library. The depression was on, and my mother favored the library over the Carlton, the Strand, and the Hunting. You know the offensive type which says, "No, but I've read the book." I've long been an offender through this simple circumstance.

Anyway, the whole scheme made me privy to extended conversations by Mrs. Capen, Miss Hines, and Miss Munsing. All three thought Governor Smith shouldn't happen to this fine, Christian country, and President Hoover should happen to it a second time. It always struck me that these painfully audible conversations were unfair to the taxpayer when he was trying to read, especially since he couldn't get into the argument.

One day I heard Miss Hines remark, on a preacher of the gospel whom she had heard the day before, "No, I didn't care for him. He had no message." Now, that phrase stuck in my memory. I was already well acquainted with the slander against Protestant worship that "all they have is the sermon" (as we Catholics used to put it), and this scrap of conversation confirmed my worst suspicions. I know a few Catholic priests by that time who "had no message" in Miss Hines' sense, but I thought that that was different.

Why did I think it was different, aside from a general conditioning in a spirit of mild polemic in my own faith-tradition?

* First published in *Jesus Christ Reforms His Church*, The Liturgical Conference, Washington, D.C., 1966, pp. 125–131.

Well, first, I had no notion that the word, "message" was a New Testament term for the word of salvation, the gospel of Jesus Christ: *lógos* or *kérygma* in the inspired original, *verbum, praedicatio* in the Latin Vulgate version. I thought it was Protestant-speak for any pulpit preaching. In the New Testament sense, the minister *had* a message; he either did not draw upon it or did not transmit it in a way to suit one hearer. Both he and his priestly opposite numbers, equally, had a "message" in the New Testament sense. Secondly, however, I thought that our priests at St. James' had a message, even though they didn't preach very often or very well; they didn't preach effectively because they didn't need to, was my youthful supposition. They did what it was proper to do in church about our Catholic faith, every time they offered Mass. You *learned* about that faith in school—at times from the same priest who did not preach very often, or very well, in church.

I am a little older now, if not much wiser. I have since learned that I was right in thinking that in their liturgical conduct the priests of my youth had a message: they "proclaimed the death of the Lord until he come." (1 Cor. 11, 26) At the same time, they did *not* have a message in the sense that they frequently failed to make a remembrance of his death through the *full* sign of word and deed: I mean the liturgy of the Word and the liturgy of the Eucharist. They unquestionably made such a remembrance, but not through its full sign. This truncation— whether it consisted in the omission of the epistle-reading in English, or of the sermon, or of an invitation to us to have any active part in the proceedings—offended seriously against the nature of the rite. Because it did, the rite failed to nourish the faith of many. In retrospect, one can absolve those good priests, and they *were* good, almost totally. It wasn't so much that preaching God's word had become a lost art in the Catholic communion: many Protestants will generalize, saying that among them the case is not greatly different. No, the difficulty went

139

deeper. It was this: that while the statement of St. Paul that faith comes through hearing was never denied, "hearing" was so widely interpreted as to mean practically every medium but the one St. Paul intended. Faith came through reading, through school-teaching, through catechizing, in very way under the sun but the Bible intelligently read out and commented upon, and the mystery of faith meaningfully celebrated. When St. Paul's context is the hearer who is not yet a believer, he cannot be speaking of God's word as it comes to us in the liturgy, but *hearer* he does say and does mean. (Rom. 10, 14) He means it especially when he speaks about faith deep in the Christian heart and praise on Christian lips. (v. 10) For him there is no avenue to such faith except the word of God proclaimed in human hearing. This is done, we know from Paul's writings, both in spoken word and in that other great means of communication, symbol or sign: the bread and the cup, the water of regeneration, the great mystery whereby a man cherishes his wife as he does his own body.

There is a sense in which the Church has only one celebration—Easter. In this view, each Sunday is but a repetition of that festival. The Christian preacher likewise has only one sermon. It is about the death of Jesus in pain and his being raised up in glory, and about the Church's union with him in this deed of God to save us. Every passage of Scripture read or homily preached must somehow throw light on the basic message that Christ "was delivered to death for our misdeeds and raised to life to justify us." (Rom. 4, 25) The reason is that each gospel selection read—and I mean by "gospel" the whole New Testament and indeed each Old Testament passage, since all prepare for the gospel—each reading illustrates one aspect of man's passage from death to life in Jesus Christ. This passage it is the preacher's task to proclaim. He calls every listener to be joined to the limited, concrete aspect of Christ's victory that is celebrated on

140

this Sunday or this feast day, through these texts of Scripture that are read out this day.

In approaching the question of the reading of Scripture and preaching, I should like to engage in a consideration or two on the relation of word and sacrament.

The liturgy of the Word, which the homily at Mass brings to a conclusion, is a proclamation of what is to happen in the second half, the liturgy of the Eucharist; it is a call to participate in it through faith. This is the inner link between the two parts of the Mass, making of it a single celebration. Neither is more important to us than the other; both must work together if God is to speak to us and we are to speak to Him in return. A better way to express this might be to say that throughout the liturgy God addresses a word to us in His Son, and patiently waits for an answer. Needless to say, He does not only speak to us within the confines of the sacramental situation. Our whole lives—our good times and bad, our successes and our setbacks, in a special way our suffering and our pain—are His word to us, if we will hear Him. Similarly, we attempt to communicate with Him chiefly through deeds of love and obedience, through service, which is the great tongue with which we call Him "Father." We will find a voice in the liturgy if we have tried to call God "Father" in all that we do. If we have not been obedient servants, our ritual behavior will be so much false posturing—mummery. He will speak to us through the medium of the liturgy if, in fact, we have let Him speak to us in our dealings with our brothers. If these conditions of love and service are fulfilled, we have in the liturgy a language perfectly suited for a conversation. Those who already have something in common converse. Others simply talk. Those who talk seem to understand each other, and this is the great deceit when people have a language but no deep experiences in common. The liturgy is a language suited to those who bring to it the "spiritual service" of a life lived. To others—to men who live but do not

141

love, who say they believe but do not serve—liturgy or rite can be the most deceptive of all means of communication.

In ancient times, the oil of the olive tree had a special message for man: it was a cash crop. As ointment it protected the face from the sun's fierce strength; it was the housewife's friend in the preparation of food. Oil is another kind of sign to us now, but from deep below the earth's surface. It is the moving force of our entire civilization. Now this cultural difference in the use of oil illustrates, I think, the difficulties we encounter in the symbolism of all our Christian rites. Olive oil, which does not figure in the lives of many living Americans, has a place in the liturgy. Petroleum, great modern sign of power, has none. Bread remains life's staple, though it be a rice cake rather than a wheaten loaf. Wine holds its own wherever grapes are grown. God uses as a "tongue" to address us what once were common, everyday things.

The "risk" He runs in all this use of symbols to speak to us is that we will no longer have understood the tongue, that we will have forgotten the meaning of the symbols.

God's answer to the problem of symbolism is that He speaks to us through sacred books that are an encyclopedia of signs, the books of the Bible. The Church never celebrates the mystery of Christ in symbol without first reading from the Holy Books. These Scriptures supply meaning when otherwise the symbolism of rite might be painfully obscure. Still, the problem largely remains. Our symbolic behavior in worship should be clarified by the Bible, but often the Bible speaks in terms of customs, practices, modes of writing that we understand no better than the signs themselves. I don't mean easy agricultural notions like "sowing" and "reaping," which we can take in even though we are not farmers. I mean ideas like that of human solidarity under the headship of one man, whether Adam or Christ, or the use of rabbinic allegory, like that of Sara's two sons, to make clear the relation between Jew and Gentile.

142

The celebrant concludes a particularly knotty passage, let us say a parable of the Savior, or Paul on the relation of the Law and the gospel. The worshipers think fleetingly, "I wonder what he'll make of that!" Often the homilist chooses to make nothing out of it, but to speak on backbiting, slander, and lies. At other times he will transpose the reading immediately into a modern key, and derive such a pat little moralization from it that the hearer is tempted to say, "I don't know what our Lord or St. Paul was getting at—but I'm sure that it wasn't that!"

The Church is committed to speaking God's word to man, and making answer, in the period between Christ's first coming and His second. That is the Church's entire vocation. We must take in a word of God that can change us. The infinite God can address us successfully only by way of accommodation. He has always leaned over in affection, as a parent to a child, to speak in language we can take in. Patriarchs, prophets, the Son of Man himself, what more could He do to speak to us in a human way? He could do one thing more, and in fact has done it. He has treated our lives and our experience fully seriously. It was a good thing to be an ancient Israelite, but it is not a good thing for us. You and I are men of faith, but we are not men of the Bible. No more are we men of wax and wine and linen and silk. We are men of sweat and grime and taxes and government forms. We study, and we work in uncongenial circumstances, and we raise our children, and we send them through school. In all this God speaks a word to us that may help us hear and speak when a certain privileged moment comes in the eucharistic liturgy.

When we use the word "hear" we don't mean merely the process of intake through the ear. We mean a taking in of God's entire word with our entire being. The equipment ordinary people have for such a hearing includes their hopes and desires, their drives and passions, their consciousness of sin, and after a certain point in life, their intimations of mortality.

143

The question to be asked, whenever a priest or a reader turns around to read, is: "How has God acted with these people seated here, through all their lives until now?" Then, "How will he deal with them in the next ten or twelve minutes?" The dynamic rubric that attends all Scripture reading is: What actually happened? What did God do next in the midst of his people? What was Jesus' saving word, His healing touch, then, that it may prove effective now?

If the reading is always about a man who prepared a great wedding feast, about a dead boy of Naim the only son of his mother, about Peter, James and John, no hearer can be expected to care until he sees in what sense all this happened to him.

The burden the hearer bears defines the homilist's task. The speaker must help the hearers identify themselves with the men of the Bible. There can be no such identification historically or culturally. It can only be done at the level of faith. But faith operates at the level of humanity—humanity integrated, uplifted, healed. The only worthwhile concerns in a homily, therefore, are genuinely human concerns. Because this is so, he who would explore God's word with his brothers must know the life they live. Civic life, the arts, work, the daily crises that mark life on the globe: these are not cheap, illustrative devices to gain the hearer's attention. They are life. Life as it is lived. Life as men know it.

Vulgarity or crudeness does not embellish God's word—though often he speaks to us through the vulgar and the crude. People have certain sensibilities about public worship which are not to be lightly tampered with. They need to know, however, that God is interested in many more things than religion, as Simone Weil once said. The renderings of the New Testament passages in our new lectionary may be a case in point. I shall not defend every last phrase, but I shall point out that the English comes perilously close to saying what the evangelists said in Greek. Many cannot endure that thought. The essence of religion for them is precisely that it is unlike life—a refuge from life—and here you have the Jerusalem crowds shouting abusively after Jesus as if he were just another "fellow" like us. The whole business is frightening. It begins to provide some idea of what the incarnation was about, and that is a terrifying prospect for many.

Do we ask for conflicting things when we specify the various ways in which faith must come to men through "hearing"? Stately movements, great music, clear speech—plus the breaking in on this hour of the life of the world in all its seaminess, its war-making, its senseless pain and crazy pleasure?

We hope there is conflict here, tension, unease, only as life is conflicting, uneasy. For the whole business of liturgy is worldly holiness—the making holy of this world—and liturgy is off to a bad start if it doesn't seem to know much about this world, or wants to create a private world of its own.

There is a very satisfying kind of sight and sound and hearing which we call religiosity. It has no bearing whatever on the great problem of life—which is to be a man of faith.

14.

ENGLISH LITERATURE ON THE HOMILY*

WHILE LITERATURE on preaching in English is fairly copious, treatment of the homily as part of the liturgy is far less abundant.[1] The reasons should be obvious to all. The Roman Catholic community—theologians, preachers, and congregations—has tended to put a relatively low value on the proclaimed Word in its insistence on sacramental efficacy. At the same time, only a halting progress has been made in understanding the true working of the sacraments; otherwise a theology of the Word would have been developed concurrently. With the rediscovery of the sacraments as signs of faith and worshipful celebrations

* First published in *The Dynamism of Biblical Tradition, Concilium*, vol. 20, New York, 1967, pp. 124–130.

[1] Some of the Catholic writing available in translation which is proving helpful in the preparation of homilies would include: W. Bulst, *Revelation*, New York, 1964; D. Grasso, *Proclaiming God's Message*, Notre Dame, 1965 (undoubtedly the best single treatment of the theology of preaching); P. Hitz, *To Preach the Gospel*, New York, 1963; T. Maertens, *Bible Themes*, 2 vols., Notre Dame, 1966; T. Maertens and J. Frisque, *Guide for the Christian Assembly*, 5 vols., Notre Dame (a rich source book which provides "exegesis, liturgical analysis, a biblical theme, and doctrine" in conjunction with each of the Sundays and major feasts); G. Michonneau and F. Varillon, *From Pulpit to People*, Westminster, 1965; A. G. Martimort *et al.*, *The Liturgy and the Word of God*, Collegeville, 1959; O. Semmelroth, *The Preaching Word*, New York, 1965; H. Urs von Balthasar, *Word and Revelation*, New York, 1964, and *Word and Redemption*, New York, 1965.

Some Protestant titles of value include: J.-J. von Allmen, *Preaching and Congregation*, London and Richmond, 1962; K. Barth, *The Preaching of the Gospel*, Philadelphia, 1963; W. Hahn, *Worship and Congregation*, London and Richmond, 1963; D. Ritschl, *A Theology of Proclamation*, Richmond, 1960; G. Wingren, *The Living Word*, Philadelphia, 1965, and *Gospel and Church*, Philadelphia, 1965.

of God's Word, an awareness of the importance of verbal proclamation as part of the "full sign" of Christ has begun to develop.

All this is to say that the fate of the homily in English-speaking countries has paralleled that of the liturgy, which in turn has depended directly on progress in the theology of Word and sacrament. Several decades of pre-theological groundwork in biblical exegesis were necessary before the inspired books could be seen in their true light: namely, as God's Word to man first delivered in a context of man's prayerful reflection on his deeds. The critical study of scripture in the Catholic Church was the pre-condition for knowing intimately its character as proclamation anticipatory of covenanted praise.

It is hard to date the beginnings of a ground swell in English-language writing, but one feels safe in naming the appearance of a slim volume by C. H. Dodd in 1936 as a major factor in understanding the homily.[2] In his concern for exegetical preaching, in which he was joined by the Reverend Sir Edwyn Hoskyns,[3] Dodd restored to the English-speaking theological community "the distinctively biblical dimensions of grace, sin and eschatology."[4] The idea of the kingdom of God returned to Christian consciousness as the apostolic proclamation of the life, death, resurrection, and ascension of Christ, which the Church makes *anámnēsis* of in a sacred meal. No longer could one misconceive the kingdom as a "future event or utopia," much less as the "sum total of decent cooperative human ventures to estab-

[2] *The Apostolic Preaching and Its Developments*, New York, 1962, and London, 1963; see also his *The Parables of the Kingdom*, London, 1935, and (rev. ed.) New York, 1961, and *According to the Scriptures: The Sub-Structure of New Testament Theology*, London, 1952, and New York, 1953.

[3] *Cambridge Sermons*, New York, 1938.

[4] H. Davies, *Varieties of English Preaching 1900–1960*, Englewood Cliffs, 1963, p. 27. This book discusses J. H. Jewett, G. Studdert Kennedy, Ronald Knox, and H. H. Farmer among others and deals with the homily only obliquely.

147

lish a more humane society."[5] Dodd's exegesis revealed the kingdom in its New Testament sources as the rule of God actual-
ized in every age by the power of His judging and saving
Word. It is helpful to recall that Bultmann and Tillich, two
theologians who insist on the "Christ-event" as that historically
given, unpredictable happening which creates the community of
the Church, are greatly concerned with preaching.[6] Dodd's stress
is on the beginning of God's mighty, saving act with Christ's
coming. Eschatology is "realized" in that the work of salvation
is achieved in the cross and resurrection; the last times are an
event of now. "This world has become the scene of a divine
drama in which the eternal issues are laid bare. It is the hour
of decision."[7] The witness given to Christ's saving act over the
ages is itself a part of the act of salvation. God's work in Christ
both is, and is not, complete.

While this fruit of New Testament scholarship—basically an
analysis of the *kērygma* as found in Acts, the Pauline epistles
and the gospels—was reaching a Protestant readership, something
like it was being made available to Catholics of German language in the "theology of proclamation" which J. A. Jungmann
contrasted with the speculative theology of the seminary
course. Neither stream was reaching the Catholic English-
speaking homilist of the 1930's, however. Such relief as the
preacher got from the wastes of his own theological formation
came with the writings of Scheeben, Mersch, Lagrange, the
Beuron and Maria Laach schools in translation, and a few pio-
neers in English like Clifford, Marmion, Michel, Vonier, and
Reinhold (the latter two, significantly, German-born). The
periodicals for clerical consumption in English-speaking countries
were not particularly helpful with respect to the homily except for

[5] *Ibid.*
[6] Cf. R. Bultmann, *This World and the Beyond,* New York, 1960; P.
Tillich, *The New Being,* New York, 1955. Bultmann's dictum is: "Preaching
itself belongs to the history of redemption."
[7] Dodd, *Parables,* rev. ed., p. 159.

148

Orate Fratres (title changed to *Worship* in 1951). Many periodicals which had a homiletic concern did positive harm through the restricted theological outlook of those who wrote about preaching in their pages. A unique English-language book in the 1940's was Martin Hellriegel's collection of homilies which interwove the texts of each day's Mass.[8]

Of the Catholics who published sermons in English from the 1930's through the 1950's, Bede Jarrett[9] and Ronald Knox[10] were unquestionably the most literate, though neither was a homilist properly so called. Knox published a small collection of expositions of the parables in the patristic rather than the modern scientific mold.[11]

One finds in English-speaking Catholic homilists of the period only a faint echo of Reginald Fuller's demand, in his important monograph on the homily, that it "build up (*oikodo-mein*) the Church . . . . [and] draw [a man] anew into the *ecclesia*. For unless the sermon leads to the liturgical action the *ecclesia* does not go on to express itself as the *ecclesia*."[12] Only biblical preaching can produce the worshiping community afresh each time, says Fuller. Neither intellectualism, nor moralism, nor emotionalism can accomplish it. In his insistence on man's need to accept in faith the event of the redemption, Fuller writes against "relevance": "Our chief concern must be not the people's needs but the Gospel in its fullness."[13]

[8] *The True Vine and Its Branches,* Vol. 1, "The Vine," St. Louis, 1948.

[9] *Lourdes Interpreted by the Salve Regina,* Westminster, 1945; *The House of Gold. Lenten Sermons,* London, 1954.

[10] *Occasional Sermons,* London and New York, 1960; *The Pastoral Sermons of Ronald A. Knox,* London and New York, 1960; *University and Anglican Sermoons,* London and New York, 1963.

[11] *The Mystery of the Kingdom and Other Sermons,* London and New York, 1952.

[12] *What Is Liturgical Preaching?,* London, 1957, p. 11. A similar distinction is made by C. Davis, "The Theology of Preaching," in *Preaching,* ed. R. Drury, Dublin and New York, 1962. Davis says that preaching is a ministry which serves faith, while the sacraments which presuppose faith are "correlative to sanctification" (p. 12).

[13] *Op. cit.,* p. 17. Like Barth, Fuller rules out all but the biblical Word.

The homily is of the genus *paráklēsis,* a deepening of the *kérygma* and *didachē* already shared through the first preaching of the Gospel and the ethical instruction given to new converts.[14] Fuller provides examples of doctrinal and ethical epistles from the lectionary, and also the three main types of gospel *pericopae:* pronouncement stories, miracle stories and parables. In "all the miracle stories in the liturgical gospels . . . the preacher must pass from the particular miracle to the ultimate miracle of the messianic redemption which it prefigures, and thence to its representation by the act of God in holy communion."[15] He is helpful on the typology of the Old Testament, holding that the oldest liturgical usage which in turn derives from the New Testament is our best guide here. He also discusses the daily homily, saying that the scripture readings uncommented on are sufficient for the small group of "regulars" but that an exception should be made on greater feasts. In the whole enterprise, the central kerygmatic truths are to be preached on at the eucharist to elicit the response of faith, "whereas the aim of teaching [*didache*] is to secure understanding of the doctrinal, ethical and devotional implications involved in that response of faith."[16]

When God's Word comes to men at worship, it is both a divine and a human action. Robert Lechner refers to the "cultic Word." "The homily is also liturgy. Preaching within the liturgy

---

14 J. Murphy O'Connor's *Paul on Preaching,* New York, 1964, is a study of the New Testament kerygma addressed to unbelievers. G. Wingren says there is no sharp distinction to be made between missionary preaching and the moral instruction given to believers: "When preaching proclaims Christ as the example of what the believer should be, it is dealing *with the world.* Christ dwells actively in his Word, and he is made flesh in the daily service rendered in the world by those who hear his Word and obey in their actions." (*Gospel and Church,* p. 30)

15 *Op. cit.,* p. 43; cf. J. Dowdall, "Preaching and the Liturgy," in *Preaching,* pp. 26–40.

16 *Ibid.,* p. 53. C. Davis, *op. cit.,* p. 18, distinguishes between evangelization (*kerygma*) and catechesis which is "a deeper and more detailed presentation of the gospel message, with the purpose of nourishing the Christian life of believers."

is liturgy."[17] This means that it is not only worship proceeding from man upward; it is also God's incorporative and formative action making the hearers into the living Christ who is forever at work in glory redeeming us.

Karl Barth, in a series of lectures first delivered several decades ago, discusses the behavior and conduct of the Christian preacher[18] and the great tension that occurs in seeking to be totally faithful to the biblical text while giving a meaningful talk to men of today.[19] In Newman's aphorism, "Nothing that is of yesterday will preach." Barth is faithful to the nature of a homily; throughout his treatment he does not discuss a sacred discourse or even a sermon. His chief principle is that the preacher must say in his own words what the bible says in the passage chosen for proclamation.

The Instruction of September 26, 1964, commenting on Article 52 of the *Constitution on the Sacred Liturgy*, requires that a homily explain some point from the day's scripture readings or from the text of the ordinary or proper of the day, "having in mind either the feast or mystery which is being celebrated, or the particular needs of the hearers."[20] This demand points to what is perennially the greatest problem of liturgical preaching: namely, relevance. Not many English-speaking Catholic homi-

---

[17] "Liturgical Preaching," in *Preaching the Liturgical Renewal: Instructional Sermons and Homilies,* Preface by H. A. Reinhold, Washington, 1964, p. 91. This small book contains a good, compressed statement on the precise nature of the homily on pp. 45ff. Cf. C. Gavaler, "Theology of the Sermon as Part of the Mass," in *Worship* 38 (March 1964), pp. 205–207; G. Sloyan, *To Hear the Word of God: Homilies at Mass,* New York, 1965, Foreword, pp. 11–15. Probably the most complete summary of contemporary Catholic writing on the homily is W. Toohey, "Preaching and the Constitution on the Liturgy," in *Yearbook of Liturgical Studies* 5 (1964), ed. J. Miller, Collegeville, 1965, pp. 15–28. Cf. also Vol. 1, nn. 1–2 of *Preaching: A Journal of Homiletics* (Jan.–Feb. and March–April 1966).

[18] *Op. cit.,* pp. 43–55.

[19] *Ibid.,* pp. 75–77.

[20] Cf. *AAS* 56 (1964), p. 890.

lists are on the alert to the existentialist interpretation of the *kērygma* asked for by men like Heinrich Ott.[21]

If God's Word and man must meet in the homily for the up-building of the whole Church—undue emphasis being placed neither on the religious and human life of the people (subjective element) nor on the mere communication of a message (objective element)—proper balance will lie in the conviction of homilist and worshipers alike that Christ's resurrection for the redemption of humanity is the one saving Word that is relevant to men in all feasts and seasons. All homilies, therefore, are paschal. The preacher's task is to explore how this enduring relevancy can be made such in terms of a relevancy the worshiper will be aware of as he listens. This demands that the Word of God be spoken at times in the words of scripture, at other times in terms of the hearer's life situation, culture, vocabulary, and needs. The homily transposes the Word of God addressed to all men into the Word of God addressed to this worshiping congregation.[22]

21 Cf. his *Theology and Preaching*, Philadelphia, 1965, *passim*.

22 A good example of the Word of God meditated on from liturgical texts is *Notes for the Preparation of the Homily*, prepared by a committee of twenty priests in the archdiocese of New York (1966). In one sense all contained therein is relevant; in another sense none is yet relevant. For some problems of proceeding to the second stage, cf. Bishop J. Pike, *A New Look in Preaching*, New York, 1961. Two different approaches to relevance, the first staying close to biblical categories, the second transposing them to life categories more familiar to the hearer, are: K. Rahner, *Biblical Homilies*, New York, 1966, and H. Fehren, *Christ Now*, New York, 1966. The reader will observe that the above survey confines its attention largely to theoretical treatments, avoiding citations of collections of homilies.

15.

THE HOMILY: INVITATION TO THE
SACRIFICE OF PRAISE*

One is inclined to say that no question is more to the fore in the minds of thoughtful priests than, "What, exactly, *is* a homily?" Both they and their listeners are coming to see that the barometer of new life in liturgy is the quality of the preaching—that joint exploration *by priests and people* of the intelligibility of the word of God.

The Shorter Oxford English Dictionary (1955 edition; the one with 2515 pages), defines the homily as "A serious admonition; a lecture; a tedious moralizing discourse." Illustration of the latter usage is given from Act III of Shakespeare's *As You Like It.* Fortunately, what is quoted above is definition b., the *transferred* sense. Definition a. holds out considerably more hope to homilist and hearer alike, and reflects adequately the longstanding Christian tradition on this oral form: "A religious discourse addressed to a congregation; esp. a practical discourse with a view to spiritual edification." A *hómilos* is a crowd in Greek, an *ilē* that is *homoû* or troop-come-together. As a Christian crowd, it is not assembled in random fashion. These people have first been called (*ekklēsía*), then gathered or brought together (*synáxis*) by God, the Father of men, to make a joyful noise under the Lordship of Jesus. They do not, however, only sound the trumpet (Ps. 47 [46], 6) or play on stringed instruments. (Ps. 33 [32] 2) They devote themselves to hearing

* First published in *Living Worship,* The Liturgical Conference, April, 1967.

153

the apostles teach and to the common life, they break bread and they pray (cf. Acts 2, 42). In the words of the Roman liturgy, they make an *oblatio rationabilis . . .* in *sacrificium laudis,* the praise of an offering in the realm of the spirit. The hoped-for effect of this corporate prayer of praise is glory to God through the upbuilding of the Christian community, that fortifying of one another which Paul asks for regularly (cf. 1 Thess. 5, 11).

The one clear function of a homily is that it must achieve the upbuilding of community, the very making of the Church. When Paul is discussing the relative merits of the language of ecstasy ("speaking in tongues") and prophesying—to which he later adds revelation, enlightenment, and instruction—he says that, whereas the speaker in ecstasy talks to God in a way which is "good for the speaker himself," the man of prophetic speech "is talking to men, and his words have power to build." (1 Cor. 14, 3) "The prophet is worth more than the man of ecstatic speech—unless indeed he can explain its meaning, and so help to build up the community." (v. 5)

The now disbanded Vernacular Society used to use verse 16 from this chapter on the masthead of its newsletter *Amen:* "Supposing you are praising God in the language of inspiration: how will the plain man who is present be able to say 'Amen' to your thanksgiving (*eucharistía*), when he does not know what you are saying? Your prayer of thanksgiving may be all that is desired, but it is no help to the other man." (1 Cor. 14, 16–17) We shall leave to one side the question of whether the comparison between incomprehensible ecstatic speech and prayer in a language not understood by the worshipers is valid at all points. Or rather, we shall enlarge its scope by saying that what Paul is doing is equating the exercise of the prophetic office in the Church, which builds up the Church, with communicating successfully with the plain man who has come to pray.

Gabriel Vahanian, who is a deeply committed Christian in the Reformed tradition, remarks in a recent collection of essays that

St. Paul did not conform himself to the "religious exigencies of his listeners in whose vernacular he proclaimed the gospel. All of us, incidentally, would do well to ponder the experience of those who undertook the task of translating the Latin mass into the vernacular only to discover that it became even less understandable." (*No Other God*, pp. 5–6) This is not, as it might seem at first reading, a gratuitous thrust at the quality of vernacular translations. Quite the contrary! It is praise of Paul for estimating his hearers' situation in the world correctly, and on the basis of this knowledge preaching a gospel in secular terms. By so doing, the Apostle took the best precaution possible against the challenge to the gospel posed by secularism. The latter would have won the day had Paul paid tribute to every expression of religiosity current in his time, whether the manifestations were Hebrew or Greek. Any such presentation of the word of God in Christ in older religious forms would only have deepened the sacred-secular split, thereby allowing the possibility of a field-day for secularism understood as a religious scheme made up of worldly values.

No, what Paul did was prescind from those old wineskins of speech and rite and custom and pour into the fresh flasks of the world of his day the new wine of the gospel. Vahanian is not faulting Roman Catholic liturgists for the language of their rendition—he is not even speaking of it—but for the very attempt at verbal rendering. They are holding to religious forms which were fresh and secular and contemporary to living men once, but are now religious in a pejorative sense because they are past. His position is arguable and we shall not argue it here. We say "pass," for the moment, to the declaration that the present Roman rite is a dead form, however gracefully its verbal content may be translated. We do *not* say "pass" to Vahanian's more general position, which is demonstrably St. Paul's, that the genuine prophetic speech of every age is the person of Jesus Christ expressed in ways sufficiently compre-

155

hensible to the common man. That man must be able to say "Amen" in good conscience at the end of the great eucharistic prayer or else he has not been built up into the people of God become body of Christ, by what has been spoken.

This means that the homily's central importance consists in the fact that it is indisputably and in a certain sense uniquely among the elements of the eucharistic action, *Christ now.* The rite, the prayers, the symbolism of food, even—and in some sense especially—the scripture readings may fail to convey the reality of Christ's presence to certain worshipers. But a man of their time who lives a life close to their lives is able to be and say Christ to them and they to him as no form or sign, verbal or non-verbal, can do.

The high value put on preaching is as old as the New Testament itself. Domenico Grasso, in his book *Proclaiming God's Message,* summons a cloud of witnesses in support of the mediation the human word affords the word first spoken by God. It is more important than administering the sacraments, including baptism, as Jesus' speech and action testify (cf. Lk. 4, 43; Jn. 4, 2). Like the Savior, Paul left baptizing to disciples while he himself preached (cf. 1 Cor. 1, 17). The bishops of the early centuries reserved the ministry of the word to themselves, and only much later let simple priests preach. Grasso speculates that they were influenced in this by the example of Christ and Paul. St. Augustine (†430) was the first presbyter allowed to preach in Africa, an event so unusual that Pope Celestine wrote the Italian bishops warning them against the poor example set. Faith and preaching are two realities put on the same plane by the New Testament (cf. Heb. 11, 6; Rom. 10, 17). Preaching is the ordinary and normal way to spread and nurture faith. From the apostolic teacher's point of view, "We cannot possibly give up speaking of things we have seen and heard." (Acts 4, 20) St. John Chrysostom called preaching the only medicine to heal the sickness of the body of Christ. St. Gregory of Nazianz described it as the first duty of bishops. Caesarius of Arles puts failure to listen to preaching on a par with dropping the eucharistic body of Christ. St. Bernardine of Siena thought it preferable to neglect the Mass and listen to the sermon when it is impossible to do both.

On the assumption that today's priests by and large are convinced of the importance of preaching and want to preach the liturgical homilies called for by the Council, we proceed to inquire into the nature of the homily. It is not, first of all, any discourse on divine things. It is part of the liturgy: an exposition of the mysteries of faith and the guiding principles of Christian life derived from the sacred text (*CSL,* 52) or another text from the ordinary or proper of the Mass of the day which takes into account the mystery being celebrated and the particular needs of the hearers (*Instructio,* September 26, 1964). The requirement that a true homily spring from the day's texts, biblical or otherwise, has led some to suppose that a tissue of citations is its essence. Nothing could be further from the truth. Simple repetition of what has been proclaimed should be needless if readers, commentators, and congregations have already done their work well. What is needed, rather, is some insight into any major obscurities the readings may pose, a consideration of some element in them common to both or all three, and above all some help to the hearer on the meaning of the one mystery of death-resurrection (Christ's and ours), as this day's celebration by this congregation reflects it.

Frequently the biblical texts of the day's mass will do very little to highlight the paschal mystery in the lives of priest or people. Every homilist is familiar with having read and re-read all the parts of a given Mass and been unable to relate them to anything he or his people genuinely care about. There are stretches of Pauline exhortation that say little to us, successive outworn epigrams in the wisdom books, fragments of miracles or maxims in Jesus' career which can test the Christian faith

157

of hearers rather than strengthen it, because they are so foreign to their lives they are living which need redemptive interpretation.

This seeming failure of the word of God to provide its minister with the minimum inspiration needed to comment on it may be accounted for in various ways: the circumscribed character of his own activities, the poverty of his reading habits, an inability to discern the Bible's one, saving message under the various forms the message takes. In any case, he should realize the freedom he enjoys if he is to do his work as a homilist well. At no time is he the slave of the word of Scripture. He is ever the free midwife of its spirit. That means he must have great familiarity with it, know its spirit. It also indicates that he has the liberty to make substitutions in the readings whenever the daily lectionary fails his people badly. The extra-eucharistic homily should be based on non-biblical readings as well. Above all, the preacher has to realize that his task is to speak the word of God in the words, the culture, the actual life circumstances of his listeners. Karl Barth's dictum on preaching is that it should be done with the Bible in one hand and the daily newspaper in the other.

The remark of a reviewer of a recent collection of homilies is apposite here: The fact that "many of the references are already dated is not a criticism of these homilies. It is a guarantee of their authenticity as homilies." If God is not saying something to us today, revealing himself in the present, we surely cannot bear the twin burden of a revelation in the distant past and a reward in the uncertain future. Rudolf Bultmann's critics like to say of him that, in his theology, the redemption is about to take place as Dr. Bultmann strides toward the pulpit. In their witticism they are not very far from the mark. Any life happening can be described as a breaking in of God on the lives of men, but Christian preaching is that intrusion in a special way. It is Christ himself addressing his people in the Spirit on the meaning that the living bread they are about to eat can have for them. It is their invitation to insertion into the reality of the cross and Eastern morning. The tones need not be somber nor the speech patterns biblical. *The message, however, has to be that of pain mixed with joy, the authentic message of the Bible.*

A homily is intended chiefly to move the hearer to decide on a course of action. It may instruct him beforehand. The homily must be intelligent and will ordinarily be informative; it should not be didactic; it may never be doctrinaire. If there is teaching in a homily, it is there as preliminary to an invitation to an act of will. Commitment by the hearer is what is sought. Needless to say, the homilist himself must be committed to the value in question. The paradox is, the more overtly or directly he asks for a response the less chance there is that it will be given. Proposing to the hearer specific courses of action can be death to the homilist's enterprise. He has to let him work out a few questions on his own. As soon as a homily's resolution takes the form of a solution (of the congregation's problems, that is), the people begin to tune it out. Up to that point the homilist has dialogued with them—left them room to think a few thoughts of their own. Now they are "cribb'd, cabin'd and confin'd" by his exhortation to a particular course of action. They have lost their freedom to choose and with it any interest in making a choice. All good homiles end abruptly, people tend to say. What they mean is, the familiar last part is missing, that painful spelling out of every possible application of the earlier remarks. All good homilies end not abruptly but artfully, which means at the optimum point—the point where the hearer is invited to think furiously about what has just been said.

The above remarks suggest that the preacher knows when he is going to conclude and, indeed, with what words. That is quite true—but then the compleat homilist will also know the precise phrasing of his beginning and middle as well as his end. Other, more leisurely forms of discourse can proceed from the well-constructed outline, but not the liturgical homily. The reason lies in its special purpose. It is calculated to move the hearer, not in his emotions (though this is not outlawed), but in his will. If it is to do so, an absolute economy of words is indicated, carefully chosen arguments and phrases, in short the full measure of the rhetorician's art. The entire meaning of a sentence can be lost by one ill-chosen word unfamiliar to the listeners.

The homily as an acceptable form is badly threatened nowadays by men without terminal facilities. They speak two minutes' worth in seven on weekdays and twelve in twenty-one on Sundays. With all the leisure of the patristic period, they are "saying a few words" on the liturgical texts. Their people are dying from a malady called the homily.

There are only two worse diseases: the malnutrition that comes with no preaching, and the poison that comes with bad preaching.

One would like to think that by a kind of reverse Gresham's law good preaching will drive bad preaching off the market. It may well be. We are probably entertaining both extremes in our churches these days—the best and the worst preaching the American Catholic community has ever given ear to.

As to bad preaching, the only hope the people have is the genuine inner conversion of the preacher. Once he submits himself to the tyranny imposed by preparing good homilies, he will immediately set people free from the tyranny he unwittingly imposes on them. Then, his overabundant speech, his inflated periods, his pious incoherence, will yield to the word of the Lord.

16.

THE CHURCH AND CENSORSHIP*

I SPENT LAST WEEK in Rome and stayed at a hotel not far from St. Peter's Church. To walk to the basilica I had to pass the headquarters of the Congregation of the Holy Office, a large, somnolent-appearing building, like any Baroque-façaded embassy in any quarter of the world. Sleeping it is, in fact as well as appearance, this grandpapa of all schemes of thought-control, for since the convening of the Second Vatican Council it has been on the defensive, and through its prefect, Alfredo Cardinal Ottaviani, has had very little to say. He himself has been practically mute since the second session, when he began to be blamed for every coercive tactic of the Council. The Holy Office is the lineal descendant of the Roman Congregation of the Inquisition (not to be confused with the Spanish or the French inquisitions). Its announced purpose, then and now, is purity of faith—faith defined in terms of the narrow, non-historical orthodoxy, which, without too much difficulty, can be shown to be mixed with the *de facto* heterodoxy, by a Vatican II standard, of the incumbents in that office. I speak of this rather unlovely institution in the Roman Church as the epitome of all attempts to exact conformity of view in terms of the highest sanction, namely divine authority, or short of that, the supposed immediate exigencies of an apostolic community believed to be divine in origin, the Church of Jesus Christ.

It is not our concern at this time to examine the dogmas of

* Paper delivered at Hamilton College, December 4, 1965.

161

the Roman Catholic Church or those religious opinions which are deemed suspect when the dogmas serve as criteria. I shall address myself rather to the delicate question of censorship of the arts as a function of the Church, past or present. I assume special reference to the Roman Catholic Church is meant, since the thoroughgoing censorship of all the arts by various Calvinist and pietist churches has largely passed into history. Except for a few sectarian groups, inconsequential both as to numbers and influence, no Christian Church known to me other than my own is active in attempts at curbing the supposed ill effects of mass media. Various evangelical churches have staked out gambling, drinking, and dancing as their provinces, but the effective control of films, plays, books, and the graphic and plastic arts through censorship is supposed—not without reason—to be a Roman preserve.

I should immediately make a distinction between censorship of the arts and attempts at controlling hard-core pornography. The two are not unrelated; in court cases their fates are immediately linked by the defense. Still, they are not the same thing, and the Catholic Church in this country, at least, is paradoxically not identified with the struggle against the pornography industry any more than she is in the forefront against dope traffic or other organized crime. As a moral force she is known to deplore all three, but the fact is that the identification, Catholic Church—anti-pornography, is not made nearly as readily as the identification, Catholic Church—pro-censorship. We must examine a little later why this is so.

In delving into the background of the censorship question we should first observe that the initial stance of the Church or Churches is one taken in favor of human happiness, not in opposition to human liberty. It is supposed that allurements to lust will never be wanting, that they will be commercially profitable in every age, and that the general run of men deserve a modicum of protection against them, on the theory that widespread capitulation will be destructive of human happiness. So goes the first line of argument.

Now that sequence of thought is built on certain *a priori* assumptions; for example, that lust is, objectively speaking, sinful human conduct and that some of its uglier manifestations can constitute public crimes. These assumptions are questioned by large segments of our society, but it is important to recall that they were universally held as valid assumptions when the great schemes of censorious control came into use. Not only could the Church count on universal agreement as to what was immoral behavior—no matter how widespread lapses from it might have been—but the Church had the additional advantage of knowing that many sins were also reckoned as public crimes. Church or canon law and civil law were either identical or ran parallel in many parts of Christendom; civil codes of penalties had not yet extricated themselves from the scheme of sins against God and offenses against the Church and churchmen. The result was that protective schemes for the populace were as much thought of as beneficent for the eternal welfare of men as for the maintenance of good civic order. Indeed, the two were largely indistinguishable in most Christian states, though I repeat that both priests and magistrates had very few illusions about the high incidence of adultery, fornication, and even grosser vices. Nonetheless, the principle was firm: the Christian prince or parliament could count on the Church, and vice versa, to support legislation calculated to preserve public morals. Such was considered to be the joint duty of sacred and secular arms. I do not wish to paint a totally harmonious picture of Church-state relations. There never has been such, practically speaking. My sole point is that the culture was based on certain understandings held commonly by men of the Church and of the state on the preservation of public order through the control of theological writing, literature, and the arts.

The notion of the control of behavior in what were thought

163

to be crimes against the state is, of course, pre-Christian. We must fix the blame on the Roman Empire for defining what acts were contrary to *pietas,* for example the failure to practice the cult of the gods of Rome, which led to the famous "ten persecutions." When the emperors became officially Christian, the same penalties tended to be levied against Jews and later against Muslims for their failure to conform. Until very modern times no society has been easy on dissidents; toleration as a political device is of long standing, but as a principle rooted in human dignity it is of very recent origin.

The first censorship scheme in Christian times—though we use the term somewhat broadly—had to do with the lists of books which, in virtue of the listing, became the canon of Scripture. Conversely, books not so named—for example the numerous "gospels" other than those of Matthew, Mark, Luke, and John—were branded as non-apostolic in origin. Sometimes books were singled out by ecclesiastical writers or churches as "spurious" when it was thought by the orthodox that the authors of these works provided a reading of the Christian mystery at variance with the apostolic "rule of faith." In such cases the bishops or other teachers in the Church who considered themselves orthodox had no qualms about branding such works pernicious or harmful to believers. They exercised the critical faculty which we cheerfully allow to a critic who writes a slashing review: "Last night Miss Katherine Hepburn in *The Lake* ran the gamut of emotions from A to B"; Ben Jonson's *Volpone:* "O to be in England, now that Wolfit's here."

An important difference between this blacklisting of certain books and the ordinary workings of literary criticism was that the highest sanction was appealed to, namely the divine. An objective reality called "apostolic authorship" was assumed, and it was stated that a particular writing did not possess it; hence the further reality, "inspiration by the Holy Spirit," did not, from its inception, attach to it. The claim was not so much made

164

that works had no right to exist and be circulated as that they had no right to have divine authorship claimed for them. Practically, of course, the two denials came to the same thing. If a literary product was thought to be both spurious and heretically tinged, you could expect those who held this view to put all others on notice, lest they be harmed by it.

This brings us to the chief point at issue. The assumption was unchallenged throughout the early Christian period, and indeed down to modern times, that false or lascivious writings, plays, and spectacles could be harmful to the reader or the viewer. "The gladiatorial games make men bestial," it was said. "Avoid them." "The detailed portrayal of the intimacies and infidelities of the gods corrupt youth. Remove the aura of religious sanction from this *genre*. It is a cheap device to justify the same sort of conduct among men. In any case, keep these plays, these erotic verses, out of the reach of youth lest youth be harmed by them." I repeat, the relation between such literary products and youth in its impressionability, or even adulthood, was assumed rather than argued. No one came to the fore with the challenge, "Who is to say that being amused or entertained is the same as being impelled to do likewise?" Rather, it was maintained against the Christian Fathers that this was life, and youth would learn about it soon enough; or, on a political and cultural plane, it was asked whether the critics were not calling into question the absolute transcendence, hence the fitting antinomian behavior, of the gods. This argument was enough to get the hemlock down Socrates' throat, even in pagan times. He argued the question much as the Christian Fathers were later to do, and was answered by the leading men of Athens in much the same way. We might call this a religious censorship scheme in aid of the state, or at least the prevailing folkways protective of the state. Atheism, you recall, was the charge against him.

Let us return to the question of the (largely unargued)

165

character of literature and other art forms as potentially harmful. Poetry, drama, and theological writing were all in this category. Works of graphic art and sculpture largely were not. Undoubtedly erotica were being portrayed visually in that age, but the portrayals were not sufficiently widespread—the art objects being limited in number—to call for universal bans. The ancient rabbis used to forbid the pious to look on graven images; the Christian Fathers similarly had a doctrine of what may be called "custody of the eyes," but they saved their chief thunderbolts for the kinetic art forms: lewd shows, dances, and acts of perversion.

You may recall the abusive character of the polemic of the Christian Fathers against anything they thought harmful to faith or morals. Their passion took the form of almost dispassionate linguistic conventions. At the drop of a hat they would characterize an idea as "impious, blasphemous, an offense against the Holy Spirit, novel, unheard of, a scandal to the human race, odious, reprehensible, and perverse." Similarly, ways of conduct such as art or entertainment forms that displeased them were likely to be labeled "filthy, carnal, degrading, bestial, deleterious to good morals, an offense to the Creator because an attack upon His image and likeness, man."

In face of such vigorous criticism, few were left in doubt as to where Tertullian, Chrysostom, or Gregory the Great stood on the works of theology, entertainment, or art they disapproved. This verbal castigation was, at the same time, the chief means employed by churchmen to achieve their ends. Whether they sought the disregard of a particular treatise or play, or its practical repudiation, they had to rely on their damaging criticism to make the point; they could not count on any policing by the state except that of individual magistrates who were Christians after the settlement of Constantine. A notable exception was the canon of Scripture, in lists which began to be uninterruptedly the same coming from certain North African provincial councils

166

around the year 400. The result of this "fixing" of the biblical books was that all others were put in a secondary and even reprobated category. This technique of listing the acceptable or, conversely, the unacceptable, did not extend further as a Church practice. Individual authors would write against certain theologians or classicists by name, but there was no churchwide practice of censorship until the advent of printing.

One notable exception should be made. In the medieval period individual bishops, university chancellors, and even popes, tried to see to it through their decrees that the manuscripts of the Arab philosophers or of Aristotle in translation should not be lectured on or circulated. This technique was thought to be an attempt to protect the purity of faith, but enough Christian theologians recognized it as a misguided one to resist all such attempts furiously. Aquinas, for example, was a free spirit in a way that many modern Catholics and Protestants are not, after four hundred years of conditioning. He was for examining every human expression of view in his search for truth. The point is, the decision was his in conscience. He was not externally coerced by the decisions of others, though he would be concerned if wise men of the past and present tended to think some piece of writing potentially harmful to faith. I make this point about the middle ages through reference to their chief theological figure. He was quite unfamiliar in practice with any scheme of control of what he could read or think, though he knew well enough at first hand of attempts by individuals to warn of the deplorable errors contained in the writing of this or that theologian or philosopher.

It was in the late middle ages, the fifteenth and sixteenth centuries, called much after the fact the "Renaissance," with the invention of printing and the wide distribution of ideas through this new medium, that bishops and popes tried to prevent the circulation of the books they labeled heretical. Licenses to print were at first in the hands of churchmen because the

167

new printers needed capital and the churchmen had it. Also, the printers tended to be interested in ideas, which means they were primarily either humanists, or Catholics, or reformers. Each had a predominant tendency. It was possible to be a humanist and a Catholic in those troubled years; It was not so usual to be a humanist and a reformer. Some reformers like Melanchthon and Oecolampadius the Protestants, and Colet, More, and Erasmus the Catholics, combined the two roles. Luther and Calvin were the products of humanism, but they were impatient of its gains as a threat to the gospel.

My point in all this is that since the printers—whether in Venice, the low countries, Germany, or Switzerland—were both beholden to churchmen and interested in the spread of the gospel as they saw it, they were likely to need licenses to print. But the licensing notion was all tied in with capital and what was a Catholic point of view and what was a heretical one. Censorship as we know it, therefore, is a product of the sixteenth-century reform. It came to an end in the nineteenth century through the movement of extra-Church forces—secular enlightenment, that is—not through any free-speech principle of the Protestant reformers or any discipline relaxation by Catholics. It is likely to die the death in Christian circles, as Catholics and Protestants come to see how common is their cause, and jointly to understand that in Christ we are free, and that it will always be a Christian service to bring to the attention of others things that may be a potential "scandal" to them.

One detail that has not been mentioned is the Grundyism of certain Renaissance prelates which may be known to you through anecdotage (possibly Mr. Irving Stone's *The Agony and The Ecstasy*). When an influential cardinal or two succeeded in lobbying for fig leaves over the private parts of cherubs—or perhaps it was our first parents in Eden—Michelangelo capitulated as he was forced to, but later had his *giustizia poetica* by painting those prelates' faces into a mural as demons in hell. There existed strong reaction to Renaissance excesses—the artist's mistress as model of the Madonna, the bosomy Aphrodites and Cleopatras in all but coital positions. Like all reaction, this one tended to sin through defect, as the original lack of restraint offended through excess. One cannot be too exercised over earnest attempts to restore chastity to public esteem if the cankers of society were promiscuity and concubinage by its leaders, whether they were princes or churchmen. The reformer always experiences a difficulty in maintaining balance since the situation he deals with—heresy, venality, lewdness—is by definition a situation which lacks balance. The axiom, "Every action is countered by an equal and opposite reaction" is true only in physics. In human events opposite reaction is seldom if ever equal.

Two books on the modern history of censorship have been done by Roman Catholics named Norman St. John Stevas and Terrence Murphy, the latter a dissertation written for the political science faculty at Georgetown University and available under the title, *Censorship, Government and Obscenity.* Stevas views the problem totally, as a barrister might; Murphy looks at it more from the point of view of the Roman Church and its four hundred years of concern with the question. Both are perceptive enough to know that the legislation that exists on the question is largely a matter of Christian sensibilities, combined with Catholic or Protestant pressures in an almost hopeless confusion. Both realize that the long-standing concern of Christian believers cannot be declared "no-concern," either retroactively or with respect to the present. An improved mentality on the question, both from the Church side and that of the state, can only come with the increased maturity of men as believers and as citizens.

The chief influence of the Church on the arts unto good—"Church" understood broadly here to describe the various Christian communities and the synagogue—is exercised when

169

men of faith on the wide scale show an appreciation of good writing, good films, good performance in music and architecture and painting and glass. By "the Church," I do not here mean the leadership element in the Church—bishops, rabbis, presbyteries, and the like—who have administrative control of funds and discretionary power when it comes to building. That is a kind of quality control which amounts to "censorship in act." The supposition often is that these men, in virtue of their office, are "the Church." But of course, this was never true. It is theoretically false in Judaism, which in concept is a thoroughgoing democracy, and in the churches of the Protestant reform, where the "priesthood of all believers" was a watchword from the start. The same point has been made resoundingly in the Roman Catholic Church in four sessions of Vatican II. The Church is the community of all believers; it is not her hierarchy only. Consequently to speak of "the Church and censorship" in terms of leading churchmen only is false to the theory of the synagogue and all the Christian churches. It is realistic and true to the facts, however, in the sense that the clergy are salaried people who can devote their full attention to affairs of the Church, and who have a well-developed sense of corporate self-preservation.

Let us look at the theory of censorship against a religious and specifically a Christian background. First, we are our brother's keeper. The Christian response to the ancient rhetorical question of Cain is, "Yes." We have a care, one for another. Second, we are not our brother's captor—his jailer or guardian. Third, we are his educator, in the sense that all of us are in the common venture of exploring the full meaning of humanity. Only one lifetime is given us to do it. Fourth and last, each of us has the guaranteed political right in a non-corporate state to damn ourselves to hell by the religious canons of another believer or of fellow believers. We have no guaranteed political right to drive cars while drunk, to smoke pot or take heroin, to rape women or molest children. A citizen of this republic may lie in bed dreaming lubricious dreams of naked women in high heels. Of his moral condition God only is his judge. But as soon as the citizens of this republic think there is some established connection between constant casual references to extra-marital sex in films and television and illegitimate births which become a public charge, or hard-core pornography and the rape-murder and dismemberment of young women, they are able to act democratically to curb what they think is a contributing cause to these effects. They may be wrong in assuming the cause-effect relation. Still, any citizenry can act democratically to protect its corporate existence or the lives and other rights of its members. At the same time, it must infringe as little as possible on the civil rights of those who are subject to coercive action.

The two examples I have taken are much too simple, of course. They are fairly self-evident cases at either end of the spectrum. A man's private sins are his own affairs in the body politic (though this is precisely not the case in the people of God or the body of Christ; there, a transcendent principle of mutual concern is at work, which does not, however, destroy privacy or the ultimate right to self-determination). A man's public crimes are everyone's concern. For these, every therapy must be explored, including attention to the external stimuli which give any evidence of aggravating emotional pathologies.

I have not yet referred to any cases that are less than self-evident. Shall the state of Maryland, for example, have a single salaried employee, expert neither in divinity nor in esthetics, as the last arbiter of movies to be shown in that state, as was the case up to a few years ago? Shall the city of Boston in the county of Middlesex depend on three persons to decide which stage plays will be shown in that city? What guidelines shall be given to Mr. Lawrence O'Brien, the postmaster general? Mr.

171

Arthur Summerfield, President Eisenhower's supervisor of the mails, tried a hard line and could not make it stick.

The adventures of the churches in these areas, and especially of the Roman Church, tend to be well reported, and a little ludicrous in their net effect. There was Cardinal Ritter and *The French Line,* Cardinal Spellman and *Baby Doll,* Fr. Hesburgh and *John Goldfarb Won't You Please Come Home?* Each acted innocently and earnestly enough in attempts to bring to the attention of Catholics in particular, and anyone else who would listen, the demerits of three questionable performances. The first two were acting as moral teachers, a role they legitimately have in the Church; the last named as the president of a ridiculed university. Their action can be interpreted as one of economic boycott and challenged on that level, but at bottom they were trying to sharpen the moral sensitivities of the general movie-going public. The attempt to teach persons like Billy Wilder or Otto Preminger a lesson is a side issue, and probably a lost cause. I am quite willing to admit that this too was being tried. From any point of view, it is a lost cause.

Can the Church legitimately do anything in the area of the censorship of mass media? My answer is that in a democracy it can do nothing in this area, legitimately. It is likely to be identified immediately as a pressure group, and this identification the Church can ill afford. All its legitimate pressures are moral, hence are exerted by conscience from within. At no point is God or Jesus Christ to be invoked as the moral monitor of those who will not accept the one as their Father or the other as their Brother. Once Christians become a pressure group they have lost all identity with their Master. Stern judge though He is of those who believe in Him, He is not to be invoked as a threatening figure in the lives of those who cannot credit Him as their Savior or their moral teacher. Neither is God the Creator to be used to intimidate those who do not see any relation of creaturehood to Him.

172

What the Church can do is help its own members form their consciences, both esthetic and moral, in such a way that they will be great protagonists of the arts, and at the same time the sworn enemies of the cheap, the shoddy, and the inauthentic. The Church has a right to expect that its sons and daughters will accept their responsibility as citizens. Whether as voters or as elected representatives, Christians will raise their voices in questions that can correctly be described as matters of public morality: war and peace, homosexuality in public places, capital punishment and other penal questions, and the general effect of mass media on public conduct. The last-named matter is one of public concern. It is simply false to declare it a private question, saying to the Church at the same time, "hands off." Our whole national public school effort is a calculated attempt to transmit a heritage, refine the human spirit, prepare the young for the responsibilities of life and citizenship. We do not regret our national stake in education. We glory in it. Much of it must be described as ethical or moral education. As a nation, through our schools and our libraries we are deeply committed in this direction. The Christian and the Jew should be expected to care about these aspects of the national life in a special way.

Both should at the same time be sensitive to the danger of making a cosmic policeman out of the God of Abraham, of Isaac, and of Jacob—a Mrs. Grundy out of the Son of Man who came not to destroy but to fulfill. As they respect man, and have a concern for his welfare they must be total in their concern: not bullying, not destroying civil rights, not curbing human freedom —in the name of God or Jesus Christ.

173

17.

PEACE*

THE ROMAN CATHOLIC, like any Christian, is in principle deeply committed to the cause of peace. If he were asked whether Jesus of Nazareth was a peaceful man he would immediately reply in the affirmative. If the further question were put, whether the Christian was expected to pursue peace with all his strength, he would similarly say that he had the obligation. Yet a paradox exists. Most Catholics are of the opinion that the injunction to peace is a matter of the avoidance of strife in domestic, business, and other personal contacts, whereas they tend to think of strenuous efforts to bring war to an end as something which ill befits the Christian. Peacemaking, in other words, is thought a fitting activity at a personal level but not at a political level. There is one major exception. It is considered acceptable for the pope to engage in strenuous efforts to outlaw wars.

The paradox is more painful still. The supposition of many Catholics is that serious engagement in peacemaking activities at a national or international level is a sign of disloyalty to their country and indeed a vice opposed to the virtue of patriotism. We should, perhaps, confine our remarks to the Catholics of the United States, for those who reside in lands which have been the scene of wars—as this country has not since 1864—are

* First published in *Spiritual Life,* vol. 13, no. 4, Winter, 1967, 231–243.

much more earnestly committed to efforts at political peacemaking than we.

We have said that when the pope publishes pleas for a cessation of hostilities it is acceptable behavior. A Catholic would not feel at home in a Church in which papal peace pleas were not issued with regularity. Ever since the days of Benedict XV the newspapers and other media have carried accounts of impassioned appeals for an end to acts of war, present and future, emanating from the Vatican. But when Pope Paul VI came to the United States as its guest two years ago there was apprehension in the hearts of many U.S. Catholics that he would "enter politics" by asking this country to pull out of the Vietnam war. Two years ago the Vietnam war was much more popular in this country than it is today. Even today, one has the impression that it is a much more popular conflict with the Catholics of this country than with this country's citizens generally. When we speak of a war as being in any sense "popular" with Christians, we have identified not a paradox but a genuine impossibility in the life of the Church. The whole question deserves some examination.

The reflections that follow will not be devoted to the rights and wrongs of the war in Vietnam. If any reader becomes emotionally disturbed over the introduction of that conflict into these pages he will not be in the best condition—or indeed in any condition—to learn about the relation of Jesus Christ and His gospel of peace to political peace in the world of men. All of us face life's major questions on the basis of certain intellectual convictions, which in turn are accompanied by emotional resonances. One need not desert his convictions nor deny his emotions in facing the problems which accompany accepting that peace which Jesus offers as His gift.

THE UNIQUE PEACE

The Savior described His peace as one which the world cannot give. This phrase cannot be meant to describe an ethereal or transcendent peace unrelated to life in the world. The ultimate source of the peace He gives us is His Father. From Him Jesus receives all that the Father has. Much of this He is able to transmit to us. Peace is a gift from Jesus Christ to men, and although it is heavenly in its origins it has to do with the harmony or discord men experience on earth. The context of peace or the absence of peace may be personal or familial, tribal or civic, national or international. Whatever the case, it is very much a matter of earth even though it is a gift from on high. We shall be examining shortly what the terms of the gift of peace are.

Peace for the ancient Israelite was the gift of his God Yahweh. Yahweh, or "the Lord," was at peace and He willed that His people should be at peace. In the early desert days He was conceived to be a conquering God of armies. He was likewise thought to be an avenging God, a God of strife in the sense that He cracked the heads of those who did not submit to His sway. This is the way He was conceived in imagery, mind you, not the way He was. The Bible speaks of God as He was known to a particular, ancient people. The only way they could know Him was through their history as a people and through the interpretation put on it by their great figures filled with religious insight, the patriarchs and prophets. These men thought of God as being at peace in Himself, but achieving peace for others by way of conquest in battle.

Certain readers of these pages know the Old Testament very well. They, above all, will realize how ambivalent it is on the question of bloodshed and peace. There is much violence reported on the sacred pages. The early murder of Abel by his brother Cain is reprobated strongly. Lamech is spoken of disparagingly, immediately after the story of Cain, because of his vengeful exploits. He was a bigamist and a bully, and the author of *Genesis* 4 has no kind words for him. Yet the conquest of Canaan by Israel is described in the books of Joshua and Judges in detail, and the warlike deeds of the Israelites are praised at every point, not reprobated. This conquest which lasted over many decades—in a sense several centuries—was not a liturgical movement. It was a methodical campaign of sacking and pillaging in which the land was possessed encampment by encampment, town by town. The all but instant victory reported in accounts such as those of the fall of Jericho and Hai is unquestionably a romanticized version. The whole bloody business was accompanied by hangings, burnings, the putting of women and children to the sword, and the sowing of whole villages with saltpeter after they had been leveled, so that no vegetation could grow there again. This technique of total demolition is known in Hebrew as *herem*—"the ban." The honor of Yahweh demanded that no one be spared, since if any of these despised pagans lived they could only be expected to return to idolatrous conduct.

The brutal conduct of ancient Israel is readily enough explained to anyone who is at home in cultural history and the *mores* of the world of four and three thousand years ago. There was much savagery abroad in those days. The people Israel was part of the ancient world and did not escape its savagery. Certain Christian readers of the Bible have a painful problem in this area because of their biblical fundamentalism. They think that the Bible is a book of moral teaching in the spirit of Jesus Christ throughout. It is not that, of course, and anyone is badly betrayed who has been led to think so. The Bible is the record of a people over many centuries—a hot-blooded, demonstrative, Oriental people which had a great conception of God and which came to be purified in its moral life, both personal and political,

177

as it let the implications of its concept of God affect its conduct. Often enough the Israelites did not see what the effect of the holiness of Yahweh on their conduct should be. Often, too, they saw but resisted the logic of what they saw. They did not let His person have the effect on them He clearly wanted to have, and this resistance the Bible calls "sin." War and violence are reprobated in the Bible, if by Bible we understand both testaments of Scripture. The moral purification of the lives of the men of the Bible was a continuing matter. It was brought to completion only with the teaching of Jesus and his gospel of peace. Still, the Old Testament is not in the first place a record of holy wars or violence in Yahweh's name. It is before all else a call to holiness and peace, a peace of which God is the author.

This peace is called in the Bible *shalom* (translated in the New Testament by the Greek *eirēnē*). Many readers will recognize the word *shalom* as a greeting, or the title of a Hebrew song. Some will be familiar with it as part of the name of a neighborhood synagogue. A Russian Jewish author named Rabinowitz who wrote earlier in this century used the pen name Sholom Aleichem, which is the ordinary Hebrew greeting "peace be to you." The Arabic cognate of this word is *salaam*—the greeting of Muslim peoples. The word Islam is normally translated "submission," meaning "to the will of God," from the verb *aslama,* "to surrender." The Muslim is committed to submission to God's will; all who are believers in the true God are committed to the idea of peace through surrender. When Luke's gospel tells of the angel's greeting to Mary at Nazareth, the Greek word found in the gospel is *chaire,* literally, "Rejoice!" (in English, "Hail"). The word that ordinarily would have been spoken to Mary was *shalom.*

The Harmony of Peace

Peace is not the same thing in the Hebrew as in the Greek world. The peace of Greece resulted from harmony and order, the "music of the spheres." Our English watchword about neatness, "A place for everything and everything in its place," describes the harmony of the Greek cosmos. Roman peace on the other hand (*pax Romana*) came as the result of administrative ingenuity. It was based on consulting the will of the peoples governed insofar as this was feasible. Roman peace was a triumph of practical reason, even as Hellenic peace was a triumph of theoretical, aesthetic concern.

Peace for the Hebrew, still another matter, is the result of the personal will of Yahweh in man's regard. It is His benevolence or well-wishing whereby He both orders all to go well with us and sees to it that it will go well. When one Jew, Muslim, or Christian hails another with the greeting, "Peace," he is asking God to enter into that other's life. He is at the same time indicating that he means to be there too, insuring the conditions of peace.

It is possible to quote Old Testament passages at length in an attempt to establish that war is or is not a defensible practice, but such proof-text exchange is in the long run time lost. What the Hebrew Scriptures convey is a spirit, a trend, a drift, and that drift is unmistakably in the direction of peace. Peace is first something in men's hearts and then it is something between neighbors, whether Jew and Jew or Jew and non-Jew, between any human groupings or factions. In the early portions of the Bible it is inconceivable to the sacred writers that the peace of Yahweh could rest on any but those who worshiped Him. Only gradually did they come to realize that His peace was a gift to those who would receive it and not to all men of Israelite stock. The prophets were so audacious as to say that Israel was at times

179

not a fit subject for Yahweh's peace, whereas the heathen were. When Jesus was preaching a gospel of peace available to Jew and non-Jew alike, He was in the line of the prophets who had rejected narrow nationalism and become a reproach to their own people with their message of holiness for all.

The New Testament attributes to Jesus, at least by implication, the Isaian title *Sar Shalom,* "Prince of Peace." Jesus is undoubtedly a man of peace, even though He does not hesitate on one occasion to say He has come to bring not peace but the sword. He divides, it is true; He separates households, setting daughter against mother and mother against daughter, among others, but only in order to reconcile and heal and fuse into one. The peace which Jesus brings is not cheaply bought. It has a price and a high one. He does not espouse living in harmony despite irreconcilable ideals. His is a peace achieved after much reflection, a peace with honor. The peace of Christ is the possession of those who accept the will of the Father, not indiscriminately of those who accept it and reject it while all at the same time call on the name of the Lord.

The Spirit of Christ

The spirit of Christ is not a spirit of selfishness, avarice, or greed. He is open-hearted and open-handed. Only in such a spirit is peace available to His followers. Those who seek their own interests are not fated to be peaceful men. Jesus, in His earthly days, was anything but a bellicose man. He described himself as meek. In speech He was gentle, if forceful, at all times. Nonetheless, the gospel record is that He was capable of violence in speech and behavior. He was no stranger to wrath in a just cause. His ejection of the traders from the temple is a classic case, but He also attacked His hypocritical opponents in bitter

180

terms. He protested strongly against an unjustified blow on the face during His brief captivity, and He addressed himself to Herod and Pilate in tones of cold contempt. One does not find in Jesus an apathetic man; He is anything but a paragon of passivity. He takes action, strong and vigorous action, in causes He is convinced of.

One of His recorded sayings goes so far as to counsel His followers to take the sword: "It is different now," He said [on the eve of His capture]; "whoever has a purse had better take it with him, and his pack too; and if he has no sword, let him sell his cloak to buy one" (Lk. 22:36). Later in the garden He was to tell one of His too eager followers to put up his sword when he struck at the high priest's servant and cut off his ear. "All who take the sword die by the sword," Jesus said on that occasion (Mt. 26:51). He asked rhetorically whether His Father could not be expected to send more than twelve legions of angels to His aid, a way of indicating that His trust was in His Father rather than in a steel blade, just as Israel was expected to trust in the outstretched arm of Yahweh and not in horses and chariots. On balance, it must be said that Jesus the man of peace is by no means a model of passivity. He becomes violently active when He thinks the cause of justice is imperiled.

We are not wise to construct a theology of non-violence or thoroughgoing passive resistance on the basis of certain texts from the sermon on the mount. Such an attempt has frequently been made. Among the most famous sayings of Jesus in this regard are the following:

Do not set yourself against the man who wrongs you. If someone slaps you on the right cheek, turn and offer him your left. If a man wants to sue you for your shirt, let him have your coat as well. If a man in authority makes you go one mile, go with him two. . . . Love your enemies and pray for your persecutors. . . . If you forgive others the

181

wrongs they have done, your heavenly Father will also forgive you; but if you do not forgive others, then the wrongs you have done will not be forgiven by the Father (Mt. 39–41, 44; 6:14–15).

Each saying of Jesus on the subject of response to persecution or armed threat must be seen in the context of His entire teaching. No single statement of His is to be taken literally in all circumstances if it does not square with the rest of His utterances or His personal behavior. There is no evidence from the rest of the gospels that He was a milksop, a man of bovine placidity uninterested in His rights. The evidence is all to the contrary.

He was peaceful in an active way, working to bring about the conditions of His Father's peace in the kingdom. His emotions were pent up at certain times and released at other times. He never failed to speak in the cause of right. He always acted for what was right even though at times, as in His passion, that action was a submission. St. Paul tells us that He went to His death willingly for our sakes out of obedience to the will of his Father. He himself said that He had the power to lay down His life and to take it up again. He went to His death in the way He did, however, because in a very real sense He had no choice. He was the victim, in those dark hours, of a violence from which He shrank and which He could not humanly overcome. Despite our knowledge of His previous election to give His life freely for the sake of His brothers, we know that He let the hour of darkness overtake Him with the inexorability of that blind cruelty which overtakes any helpless victim.

The peacefulness of Jesus is a cumulative thing rather than a matter of this saying or that on the subject. We suggested above that His utterances can be made to cancel each other out, yet His words and deeds in sum do not end in a draw. There is nothing neutral or neutralizing about them. They are all in the way of peace, of intelligent, courageous action to bring about

182

the possibility of openness to this gift of God. In the interests of peace Jesus asks men to cast all bitterness out of their hearts. He requires that they give and love and serve and share. If this advice is followed it leads to the end of quarreling and depredation and murderous destruction. In a word, it brings an end to war, whether that unlovely expression of human hate is carried out on the battlefield or in the civil arena or in the church or in the home. Wars declared and undeclared, spoken and unspoken, fought with or without instruments of carnage, are brought to an end by the full acceptance of Jesus' spirit of peace.

THE CHURCH AND PEACE

The notion of the church as the great protagonist of peace on a social rather than on an individual scale came slowly, if it came at all. The development was made in halting and painful stages. In the first five centuries of the Church's life, the period of the Fathers of the Church or "patristic era," Christians were encouraged not to become soldiers. They were even forbidden by some writers to serve in armies. Frequently enough this would be because of something extrinsic to the conduct of war itself. An oath of fealty to the emperor was required which conceived him in terms of deity. Hence military service was outlawed because of its connotations of idolatry. Again army service was vigorously written against because of the evil associations possible in that life. There is no strong and clear voice of a Christian writer, however, which forbids participating in armed conflict for the precise reason that the Savior forbade it. And there is good evidence that our term "sacrament" derives from the military oath of soldiers at their induction. Tertullian in the late second and early third centuries, who is our witness for this usage, featured the fact that Christians were found everywhere. It is well known that they were found in the Roman army, and even that Christianity achieved some of its spread through this means.

The Church Fathers were silent on the subject of war for the most part until the time of Augustine. He is for all practical purposes the author of the Christian theory of the "just war," a theory he devised to meet the pressing problem of his own time of the barbarian threat to the empire. Augustine contended that because of the Christian's charity no disciple of Christ should kill in self-defense, since he should not love life or property more than God or neighbor. He went on to say that in order to maintain peace, rulers have the right, at times the duty, to make war, and their subjects have the duty to obey when the command is not clearly opposed to a law of God. Augustine proposes one legitimate reason for making war, namely the defense of peace against its serious rupture.

Even a just war must be waged in a spirit of mercy for the defeated and with peaceful intent. Three things seem to have limited the course of war in Augustine's thought: its purpose, its authority, and the way it is conducted. Despite the fact that he argued this theory, he never seemed to have satisfied himself as to the full compatibility of war with Christian charity. Various theologians developed Augustine's argument, though not very far it must be admitted. Among them were St. Thomas Aquinas and the sixteenth- and seventeenth-century theologians Vitoria and Suarez. The Augustinian argumentation has continued down to our own time, at least through the papacy of Pope Pius XII, who even in the age of atomic, bacteriological, and chemical warfare argued in 1949 that, "There are some goods of such importance for the human community that their defense against an unjust aggression is without doubt fully justified" (*AAS*, 41, 13).

The next step after Augustine in the generally unenviable Christian record on the subject was the idea of the holy war.

It cannot be denied that the Crusades were preached as a vindication of the honor of God and Christ against the infidel Turk and the Jew. A facile association was made between the Christian cause in reclaiming the holy places and the fate of the kingdom of God. Rape, burning and looting, frequently against helpless villages along the way to Palestine, were the bitter fruit of this misbegotten zeal for the gospel. The relationship between Christians and Jews and between Christians and Muslims was worsened almost beyond repair in the period of the Crusades.

The notion of freedom from serious guilt in war-making was contributed to by the medieval ideas of the shortness of earthly life and its unrealistic quality as contrasted with eternal life. Aside from the unavoidable ravages of plague, infant mortality, and fire in those days, there was a conviction abroad that there was little harm in snuffing out a man's life because he would shortly be in the hands of a just Judge anyway, where he could get started on the serious business of eternal life or eternal death. The Spanish proverb is not without relevance here, "*La vida es sueño,*" "Life is a dream."

THE SOLDIER OF CHRIST

Feudalism brought in its train the notion of the *miles Christi* or soldier of Christ who was as favorable to the cause of the Savior as one might be to a king or baron. Chivalry in its high period challenged the knight to a code of honor wherein the liege lord and gentle lady served as surrogates for Jesus and Mary. This romanticized view of the military career, while characterized by an unbending code of honor, nonetheless clothed every sort of brutal conduct in the interests of a cause thought holy. The sole beacon of hope through this bloody period of a thousand years was the development of the "peace of God" and

185

the "truce of God." These were arrangements which centered around times and seasons in which mutual destruction was briefly suspended so that men could till their fields, visit their families, or keep the Christian feasts. Nonetheless, it was a time that had no difficulty in acknowledging warrior saints such as Joan of Arc, Louis of France, and Lawrence of Brindisi. The latter, a recent "Doctor of the Church," had a better record in leading armies than in serving as a teacher. His sermons had to be resorted to in scant evidence of his designation for this honor, for the Capuchin friar was much more at home with reins in his hands than a quill.

Francis, the poor man of Assissi, was unquestionably a man of peace in the mold of Jesus of Nazareth. He went to the Holy Land out of unaffected love for the heathen. One thinks of the noble deeds of Catherine of Siena in attempting to bring Church schism to an end, and those of the bishop of Geneva, Francis of Sales, who deplored the religious wars of his day and struggled to terminate them. Nonetheless, it must be acknowledged that a churchwide commitment to peace in the Christian order did not come until the seventeenth century with its various streams of Protestant pietism. It is true that a number of medieval sects which were described as heretical at the time had a more than ordinary interest in evangelical peace. Nonetheless, it was left to various groups of evangelical brethren in Germany, the Low Countries, and England to identify themselves wholeheartedly with active resistance to war. Notable among these in the English-speaking world was George Fox's foundation, the Society of Friends or Quakers as they came to be called, who were led by an "inner light" to do the works of peace. The larger Church bodies, namely Roman Catholic, Evangelical, and Reformed (Lutheran and Calvinist, i.e.), seemed too enamored of the idea of the Christian prince who was a defender of the faith and of the alliance between throne and altar which was the residue of the Constantinian settlement of 311 A.D. to take the prophetic stance.

The Modern Church

In our time it is a commonplace and not by any means a slander to observe that the higher clergy of all the major Churches have blessed weapons, been active in support of armies, and devised theological rationales to establish why "God is on our side." They have not tended to be sympathetic to the peacemaking tradition that goes back to the great Christian saints, Catholic and Protestant, and ultimately to Jesus himself. Some have even given evidence that they think peacemaking to be the work not so much of moral weaklings as of the deluded, the naïve, those who will not come to terms with the fact of lawlessness abroad in the world. There can be no question that there is such a mystery of inquity, that demonic powers exist which are opposed to God and Christ. Paul taught that such a principle of evil existed and was being restrained, even if not perfectly, until the end of time. It is further true that patriotism is a virtue for the Christian when it does not veer by excess toward a chauvinistic spirit of narrow nationalism.

Pope Pius XII has rightly said that in an era familiar with weapons of mass destruction, failure to defend human liberties would give "free field in international relations to brutal violence and lack of conscience" (*AAS*, 45 [1953] 748). There can be no question that situations arise in the modern period in which all hope of averting war seems vain. Unjust attacks by nation upon nation have been a regular happening since the beginning of this century. Wars of self-defense marked by some hope of success and entered upon as a last resort cannot be thought of as illegal. They may, in certain circumstances, be thought of as obligatory. However, the case of the nation unjustly attacked and

187

menaced in its vital rights is not the case we speak of here. We are more concerned with the thoughtless assumption that a certain war is right because one's country happens to be engaged in it. The proposal is dismissed out of hand that grievances should be examined in endless conferences at the peace table before hostilities are declared. Rather, ultimatums are to be issued saying that the offenses of neighbor nations are to be punished, lost lands are to be recovered and expansion into roomier territory is to be sanctioned, for the reason that a nation has needs and aspirations which cannot be fulfilled within its territory.

Churchmen, it should be supposed, will be in the forefront of every action for peace. As a matter of fact, taking all of Christendom into account over the last six decades, they have a record of almost unbroken silence. Many have not hesitated to associate themselves with the war machines of their own nations. The papacy has a reasonably good record among Roman Catholics, but only since it was stripped of its temporal holdings in 1870. Certain Protestant groups, notably the World Council of Churches and the National Council of Churches of Christ in America, have made bolder declarations than anything stemming from Roman Catholic sources other than the papacy. We must ask why this is so.

The most evident reason—aside from the possible failure of Roman Catholic churchmen to be lovers of peace in the gospel sense—is that international communism has been identified as an antireligious force since the Russian Revolution of 1918 and even the European uprisings of 1848. Second only to Jews, Roman Catholics have been the major victims of communist techniques of spoliation and disenfranchisement. An easy identification has been made between the work of satan and the communist cause. The same mentality which finds conspiracy everywhere, whether of international Jewry, Freemasonry, or anti-Catholicism in its various forms, has been quick to recognize the

188

conspiratorial hand of Marxism or Stalinism everywhere. Little or no account has been taken of the aspirations of the people in communist countries to get enough to eat or to throw off the shackles of feudal oppression. Often these bonds will have been made fast by Christian sovereigns, colonial exploiters, or native landowners. Christians in this country generally have not cared to know why communist regimes have been welcome alternatives to governments in power. The formula is much too attractive which equates communist leadership with satanic power. It is a clear case of black and white for the Christian, and he chooses white. Consequently, the great bulk of Christians, and Roman Catholics in particular, are of a mentality which holds that opposition to world communism comprises a holy war in the strict sense. There is much talk of enslavement of peoples and the rights of small nations to self-determination. In fact, however, the fate of the Church as an institution is often the chief thing at issue, without any special inclination to discover whether self-determination might not end in a communist regime. The people might indeed choose one, in an attempt to improve their lot over the evils they have experienced under Christian, Buddhist, or Muslim control.

The Search for Peace

It has all too easily been supposed that active work for peace ends inevitably in laying down one's arms, following which workers' states or peoples' states will take over. One thing that the Christian must get clear, which he by and large does not have clear, is that the clamor for peace on the part of many in the Marxist sphere is quite genuine. The early means to achieve this peace are deplorable. They include what is thought to be the necessity of taking freedoms from workers so that ultimately the proletariat or greatest number of people may enjoy the

189

fullest freedom. There are serious flaws in the economics of Marxism, whether pure or developed, but in concept a state of free workers is looked forward to, not a state of the enslaved. The only meaningful response to the appeal communism has is an economic and political system which will bring more freedom to the greatest number sooner. With the exception of a few scattered instances in which governmental efforts have received Catholic sanction, the normal Catholic response to active efforts at peacemaking is an almost pathological fear of being duped by the communist world. This gives us the paradox of a Roman Catholic Church which is not thought of on any worldwide scale in connection with making or preserving world peace. The popes are our sole men of concern, practically speaking. We have arrived at a handy formula whereby we must praise all they do or say in this line; no other Catholic person is free to work for peace without having immediate opprobrium visited upon him. Catholic pacifists are few, but they are known to be men and women of courage. Their activities in demonstrating against war, in framing petitions against the current war in which the U.S. has already 100,000 killed and wounded; and draft-card burning, are looked on with suspicion by the great bulk of United States Catholics. Yet, these men and women are being faithful to the gospel of Christ as they understand it, in a way at least as courageous as that of combat soldiers. Their entire concern is to see that there are no combat soldiers. They want our finest young men out of the trenches, out of the rice-paddies more than anything else; one might even say they want it more than anyone else. For their efforts they are reviled. We cling to the conviction that the only honorable way to extricate oneself from a war is to slaughter one's way out or be slaughtered; we fear every peace but one of total victory as a dishonorable peace. We will not believe the Savior when He tells us we must be lovers of peace, understood as a gift of God to which we lay ourselves open.

190

The Instant Question

Many of our contemporaries who are neither pacifists (a technical term describing those who will not bear arms in any cause) nor Marxists are nonetheless strongly opposed to the engagement of the U.S. in the Vietnam war. They have a variety of reasons, some political, some humanitarian. Certain of these persons are not opposed to all wars but they are opposed to this one. Ranged opposite them are other thoughtful people who think most wars savage and senseless but this one justified because of its vast implications.

Where is a Christian to take his stand in this question, both of war in general and the present war? First of all, he cannot forget what he knows about history and government, hunger and tyranny. One is not required to become politically unsophisticated just because he has deep religious convictions. No, retaining all he knows about political reality and the enduring presence of evil, the Christian is by definition constrained to deplore the fact and the theory of war. It should be expected that he will be in the forefront of all attempts to achieve a lasting peace. But the first and most serious proof of this will be his concern to bring to a halt any war now in progress. He must hate war as he hates sin because it is the fruit of sin and leads to sin. He must, in a word, be a man of peace by doing the works of peace—and this he will find as unpopular a cause today as is the life of Christian virtue in any age.

18.

DEBATE ON THE EUCHARIST*

WHEN CATHOLICS READ *Mysterium Fidei* in early September 1965, or newspaper summaries of its content, they could only have had the impression that Pope Paul was taking a position somewhat counter to that of his brother bishops in their Council document, the *Constitution on the Sacred Liturgy*. It seemed to neutralize the Council Fathers' major concern for the restoration of Mass as the commemorative celebration in Christian communities of "the mystery of faith" by simply redefining it as the prayer of the Church whenever it was validly offered by a priest.

Since the latter truth had not been called in question in any circles American Catholics travel in, many wondered why the Pope had bothered to reaffirm it. Neither had Catholics been heard maintaining that the body and blood of Christ in the Eucharist were such only at the moment of their being eaten, another position reprobated in the encyclical. Denial of the first proposition and affirmation of the second would comprise heresy. It is always helpful to have errors in faith delineated, but it is puzzling to have them warned against when they are not being held by anyone one can name. The puzzlement was heightened because the Pope seemed to be hinting at heresy from the standpoint of those Catholics who were not receiving instruction in the solid eucharistic theology of Vatican II. Any who were prone to associate the eucharistic theology of the

* First published in *Commonweal*, June 17, 1966, 357–361.

constitution with unsound doctrine seemed to be receiving all the aid and comfort they needed, and from the highest source. The Council document received verbal praise in the encyclical, even to a repetition of the various modes of presence of Christ in the Mass, but there seemed to be wanting a deep understanding of its overall intent.

So things stood by the middle of September. The non-Catholic observers at the Council reconvened convinced that the Pope had set back the cause of ecumenism seriously, not by reaffirming Christ's real presence in the Eucharist but by once again making the term "transubstantiation" a condition of faith in this mystery. In fact, the encyclical reiterates this word from Trent which had spoken of it as *"convenienter et proprie, aptissime"* (correctly, very fittingly) descriptive of the mysterious change of elements (Sess. 13, ch. 4; also can. 1). The question it does not address itself to is the very one at issue, namely whether this term commits the Roman Catholic Church to a particular philosophical position in its adherence to a New Testament mystery. And if it does not, well-disposed Protestants and Orthodox asked, what is the ecumenical good sense of retaining the term when it is so widely thought (by Protestants and Catholics alike) to make a development in Aristotelian theory the substance of faith?

Immediately upon the appearance of the Pope's encyclical the Dutch bishops, through Edward Schillebeeckx, O.P., Cardinal Alfrink's Council *peritus,* stated that none of the Dutch theologians whose names had appeared in press reports could be among those under the encyclical's censure. These would include Piet Schoonenberg, S.J. and Luchesius Smits, O.F.M. Cap., both of whom repudiate in their writings the positions repudiated by the papal document. It was pointed out on the same occasion that since the Pope had acknowledged with approval a pastoral letter of the Dutch bishops of May, 1965, which censured certain imprecise pastoral teaching and practice on the Eucharist, no

193

rebuke of Dutch Catholicity was to be entertained. In fact, however, a Dutch translation of the encyclical was made available by the Vatican, an unusual move.

With the passage of the autumn months it became clearer why the Pope had warned in a Church-wide statement against errors which few in the Church had heard of. In a word, he feared that the hearers were by no means few. The Catholic press in certain countries and large circulation media like *Time* (July 2, 1965) had evidently contributed to the spread of views which needed arresting by the drastic measure of an encyclical. Chief among them was the idea that the consecrated species at Mass were not themselves the body and blood of Christ but only a sign of them; that in the context of a meal Christ is "encountered" but not in fact eaten; that He is present "to" the bread and wine but not precisely under their appearances; and that because Jesus Christ comes in the sign of a meal, He is not to be addressed in contemplative prayer or gazed upon in the form of bread.

The Pope was most emphatic that the Church's faith in the Eucharist was a faith in transubstantiation. No term is needed to improve on this one, though the intent behind the use of others was allowed. Rejection of the idea it stands for is to be attributed to weak faith in the almighty power of God. Finally, the Pope indicated that he could not conceive of a priest who would not wish to celebrate the Eucharist daily (be himself a celebrant seems to have been his meaning, though this is not said in so many words).

EARLY CHRISTIAN BACKGROUND

Now all these ideas need to be much discussed and preached about if waning faith in the chief Christian sacrament is to be avoided. The whole purpose of the liturgical renewal is to

194

increase devotion to the Eucharist. If the Church is experiencing a great numerical growth in the reception of this sacrament but no corresponding intensification of adherence to the person of Christ, that fact needs looking into. Perhaps increased commitment to His person is being achieved through the Eucharist, but at the price of unconcern for His real presence *sub specie panis et vini.*

Are visits to the Blessed Sacrament "falling off"? If so, is it because they are being actively discouraged, or at least not encouraged? What is the fate of the Forty Hours Devotion, all-day exposition, nocturnal adoration? Do these practices languish while the celebration of the Mass flourishes? If this is true, is it by way of a cause-and-effect relation? Eucharistic devotions apart from the Mass suffered no diminishment during the period 1910–1960 when the Jansenist threat of infrequent communion was being overcome. Yet the liturgical movement seems to be doing them real violence. Is this happening on any principle, or are quite other factors at work?

Many of the above matters are unresolved questions of fact. Once the importance of answering them is established, the ordinary techniques of sociological inquiry can be employed. First, however, it should be ascertained, in accord with principles of sacramental theology and the history of piety, which of them are worth seeking an answer to and which not. While all questions touching sacramental life are important, not every expression of sacramental piety is of the same importance as every other.

The sacrament of the Eucharist derives from the New Testament, where it is described as organically continuous with the worship behavior of the Old. Yahweh, God of Israel, and this people were anciently in an historical covenantal relation. The covenant was a personal, contractual arrangement whereby He unilaterally initiated unlimited benefits for them if they would be faithful to Him. Manna ("bread from heaven") was the sign

195

of His beneficence at one important point in the history of this people. At another, the covenant He made with them was sealed with the blood of heifers and goats, blood being the sign of life and fidelity.

Israel was no stranger to the universal religious custom of the sacred meal. Its chief expression was as a remembrance rite of Yahweh's bringing the people Israel to birth in the desert (the "Passover" rite). When Jesus identified His impending death and resurrection as basically an act of covenant renewal (a "new covenant in my blood"), He did so in the context of a sacred meal. It was to be a memorial (*zikkārôn, anámnēsis*) which, when eaten, would bring Him into the midst of His brothers as one freely offered to His Father.

The New Testament tradition other than that of the gospels is that this meal was taken commonly from earliest times. Two separate traditions on it were early fused, or it may be that the two chief aspects of the one mystery were discovered: the joyous recall of the Lord's resurrection whereby He continues to be present in the midst of the community, and the commemoration of His painful sufferings and death. From the time of the first Pauline churches the two notions are found in conjunction. St. Paul considers it necessary, however, to separate a Christ-commemorative meal of fellowship (*agápē*) from the strictly sacramental rite in bread and wine. The latter sacrament stands out in the New Testament as the epitome of new life in Christ. An early liturgical formula inserts the words "mystery of faith" into Jesus' words of institution over the cup. The indisputable testimony of the post-apostolic and patristic periods is that the presence of Christ in the Eucharist is unique among His various sacramental presences. He works *through* the sign of water in baptism, *through* oil in healing the sick; He is *in*, or Himself *is*, the sign of bread and wine in the Eucharist. After the priest's consecratory word in anaphora or canon, the food and drink is no longer ordinary but is reckoned as the Lord's true body and blood. No other tradition can be called authentic.

Early modes of speech about the Eucharist are not personal. The species are not spoken of as "He" but "it." The sacred food is a "type," a "figure" of Christ; the sacrament is denominated the "holy bread," the "cup of salvation," a usage retained in the Roman rite of the Mass. Still, there is no doubt that the food-stuffs are, in fact, the body and blood of the Lord. The Greek Fathers speak of changed elements (*metastoicheiōsis*) and the Latins just as firmly of complete change (*conversio*). What had been bread and wine is now the Savior, to be eaten in a remembrance rite. This food will achieve salvation for the believer who accepts in love the power of the cross and the risen life.

With the early transition in the Church from a predominantly Jewish to a Gentile membership, the primitive New Testament notion of a sacred meal sacrificial in itself underwent modification. Instead of the biblical emphasis on the meal as the essence of the rite, the Greek and Roman religious backgrounds tended to place the center of gravity in the offering or up-bearing which preceded the meal. The American theologian Kilmartin has lately shown how the classic liturgies of Byzantium and Rome not only had this characteristic but also discouraged communicating through their stress (basically that of Ambrose, Augustine, and Chrysostom) on the awesome majesty of Christ who was not to be approached thoughtlessly.

After the patristic age there came (in the eighth through eleventh centuries) an emphasis on Christ's physical real presence in the Eucharist which was quite foreign to the New Testament, the liturgies, and the Fathers. Popular teachers pointed out that with one's teeth one touched the arms and legs of Christ which had been racked on the cross. Berengarius, a priest who lived through most of the eleventh century, distinguished himself as the "first heretic of the Eucharist" by resisting this kind of

197

thing. He was made to sign a formulary drafted by a Roman synod in 1078—he subsequently recanted, then recanted the recantation—which St. Bonaventure did not hesitate to brand excessive. St. Thomas Aquinas interpreted the papal document in a more reverent spirit, then proceeded to alter its meaning substantially.

These two thinkers of the high scholastic period (and to them should be added St. Albert the Great) were busy restoring to the Eucharist the spiritual sense it had traditionally enjoyed and divesting it of the excessive realism of a physical interpretation. "Sacraments belong to the *genus* of sign," wrote St. Thomas. He declared that Christ was present in the Eucharist, "not in his proper appearance but under the appearances of this sacrament." Of the numerous bleeding hosts of his day he wrote in his theological *Summa:* "What this miraculous blood might be I know not; in any event it is not the real blood of Christ."

POPULAR EXCESSES

In their eucharistic teaching the reformers were reacting not to this genuine New Testament sacramentality but to the excesses of popular piety. Recall that the desire to receive the Lord's body at Mass had so waned by the year 1215 that the IV Lateran Council decreed the necessity of communicating once each year. The non-involvement of congregations in the liturgy had played a large part in this decline. A rite that was conceived as a sacrifice complete in itself and not as a meal came to be dealt with as such. Other benefits than nourishment began to be looked for from Christ's body really present. Chief among these advantages was the healing power to be gained from looking on the Lord's body.

It is true that adoration was the motive that led to the elevations at Mass, to the Corpus Christi procession, and to benediction with the sacred host, but the Eucharist was adored with a view to the benefits to be derived from gazing. It cannot be put too strongly that whereas reservation of the Sacrament is an ancient practice (for the sick, for communicating at home, for exchange among bishops), the various devotions in the West which center around reservation flourished as substitutes for celebrating the rite of the Mass fully, including receiving communion. This means that, *a priori,* we should not be surprised if a return to a New Testament view of this sacrament were to modify certain developments which are without a biblical history. Needless to say, a weakened faith in Christ's eucharistic presence would not be a necessary part of any such modification of practice.

The Reformers, as is well known, began by attacking eucharistic abuses. They opposed the use of the Sacrament as a talisman, and very shortly found themselves describing adoration of it as the idolatry of a bit of bread. They wanted its primitive meal character restored, and were soon holding that there could be no eucharistic reality apart from the meal. Most importantly, they so insisted on the uniqueness of Christ's sacrifice in the real order of history that they came to deny its authenticity in the real order of sign. They meant to deny that repetition in the order of historical reality was possible but many ended by denying sacramental reality as well. Not having been made sufficiently at home by Catholic teachers with a spiritual presence in sign, in which the sign of the Eucharist was mysteriously the reality signified, Christ himself, they concluded to the fact of other, lesser symbolisms.

The element common to all of these was that the command of the Savior to eat His flesh and drink His blood was fulfilled by celebrating a meal in which His spiritual presence was achieved through recall of His person and His deed. At times

199

a rational spirit may have been at work—a real skepticism with respect to the data of the senses. In the main, however, there was no lack of faith among the Reformers in God's almighty power. They were simply convinced that He had not expressed it in the way the Catholics claimed. The Catholics, in turn, were defenseless through their failure to have taught well the sacramentality of the New Testament which was their heritage. The "realism" threat to Catholic sacramental doctrine was persistent. Moreover, the failure of Trent to initiate any serious liturgical reform—vernacular tongues, rite, Eucharist under two species—was a serious handicap. The Tridentine settlement left Catholics with a firm grasp on one real presence of Christ in the Eucharist, His presence under the species, but no sound appreciation of the further, fuller presence of Christ to Christians which the Reformers were so intent on.

It is these additional presences of Christ which are at the heart of the modern controversy. The primitive Church was quite clear that the Savior had left behind Him a memorial meal as a way to be in the midst of His brothers. Meals can be highly satisfying human experiences which create a real unity among those who partake of them. For the Church, the chief effect of the Eucharist (and therefore its chief purpose) was the knitting together of the community in love. Christ was present as host and as food, but also as guest in the person of those who partook.

When this earliest view of the Eucharist had become obscured, Aquinas led in its restoration. As part of his overall concern with the true nature of sacraments, he distinguished among three elements in the Eucharist: the "sign only" (the consecrated foodstuffs), "the reality and the sign" (Christ really present under appearances), and the "reality only" (the unity of the Church). The last named reality is the ultimate one, the very reason why Christ becomes available in the sign of food. As Catholic piety customarily puts it, He is on our tongues so

200

as to be in our hearts. Christ's real presence as food achieves the purpose intended only when He is present to the believer as one person is to another. His personal presence to many individuals is, in effect, the making of the Church. This holy assembly becomes one through a common faith in Christ crucified and risen, who continues to be in its midst through His presence in this sign.

The truth of the ultimate reality of Christ's presence was retained by the Reformers at the price of His proximate presence in the sign. The Fathers of Trent repudiated belief in His presence "in sign and figure only." The unfortunate side effect of this testimony to the ancient eucharistic faith was a new Catholic distrust in symbolism, the very essence of sacramental reality. Only in this century did theologians like Beauduin, Casel, and Masure begin to restore the balance. The German monk Vonier (of Buckfast Abbey, England) was the successful popularizer of Aquinas' eucharistic teaching, while in this country H. A. Reinhold was the chief informant on a wide scale of the progress being made in European Catholic sacramental thought. The restoration of these partially forgotten truths about the nature of sacraments culminated in the spelling out in the *Constitution on the Sacred Liturgy* of the multiple presences of Christ in the Mass.

He is present there, say the Council Fathers, in the person of the celebrant, in His word (hence in the reader and the homilist as well as in the scriptures), under the sacramental species, in the prayers and songs of the rite, and in His brothers who celebrate. This being so, one correctly deduces that Christ is equally present in all Masses only in terms of one of the five real presences listed. The measure of His presence through the remaining four modes will establish the measure in which Christ, really present after the consecratory prayer, will be present to individuals and to the congregation. How well He reads and preaches and celebrates and sings, through His ministers and people, will determine how much He is received once He offers Himself in host and chalice.

TWO SIDES

This Catholic faith in the multiple real presences of Christ, newly recalled, is doubtless the cause of the tensions which led to the encyclical. Ranged on two sides are those who have never considered any eucharistic presence of Christ besides that of His really "being there" and those who are so convinced of the reasons why He is there that they tend to stress the Eucharist as a means to this end, not an end in itself. But an adorable divine Person considered in any way *but* as an end is a scandal to many—again, the result of the imperfect catechizing they have received in the mystery of the redemption.

Dr. Schillebeeckx gave a highly illuminating conference on the subject at the *Domus Mariae* in Rome on November 9, 1965. It was based on a two-part article of his in *Tijdschrift voor Theologie,* the first of which (on the meaning of "transubstantiation" at Trent) had already appeared, the second of which (on the ideas underlying the proposed terms "transignification" and "transfinalization" and their relation to Tridentine doctrine) had not. This talk was subsequently made available in mimeographed form by the Dutch Documentation Centre of the Council (DO-C). It merited the unusual attention of a disclaimer by Archbishop Felici on the Council floor of any "official" character of the talks being given there. A lecture was also delivered at the Gregorian University on December 1 by its English professor, Dr. Francis Clarke, S.J., on "The Real Presence." It was sponsored by the Cardinal of Westminster, again an unusual move by Roman standards during the Council.

Schillebeeckx reviewed a controversy of the last fifteen years between Professor Selvaggi, S.J., of the Gregorian University and the theologian Carlo Colombo of Milano, in which the former held to a "physicism" which seemed to connote chemical change in the eucharistic elements while the latter held for an "ontological" change. Schillebeeckx further explored the phenomenological character of modern philosophy, opposed alike to any Aristotelian nature theory and the "gnoseological" orientation of even the best of Scholastic sacramentality. In the latter view the chief characteristic of signs is that they convey knowledge of the thing signified rather than transmit something of its whole being. The philosophies of personalism and phenomenology together demand a more apt expression of the mystery of the Eucharist than Aristotle's metaphysics can supply.

At this point the Flemish Dominican recorded his conviction that the word "transubstantiation"—first used between 1100 and 1130—meant simply *conversio* or *transelementatio,* that is, complete change. In that primitive sense it expresses faith in the New Testament reality. By the time of Trent most of the Fathers probably thought that the philosophical teaching on substance and accident was implicated. Their ignorance on this point would not have prohibited the term's having its more general significance, however.

ONTOLOGICAL CHANGES

Schillebeeckx observed that in the debates which preceded the vote of Session 13 of Trent some bishops remarked that the term was at the same time "learned and barbarous." In any case, the reality of the eucharistic mystery is a change in the bread and wine that is total, while at the same time nothing experiential to sense is changed. He calls this change "ontological" because it affects the food-become-person in the depths of its being. The change may legitimately be called "transfinalization" or "tran-

203

signification," he said, terms which the Pope's encyclical allows. In the first case the purpose (*finis*) of bread and wine had originally been to nourish physically. Now it is to put the recipient in personal contact with Christ through His new presence. In the second, the bread and wine signified ordinary eating, the strength it gave, and the fellowship of a meal. After the change it stands for the glorified Christ, now present, and the new life which accepting Him in faith gives.

"Transubstantiation," initially, seems to give a better assurance of Catholic faith than the other two terms because the notion of "total ontological change" appears to be built into it. When the terms "transfinalization" and "transignification" are used, the end and the significance of the consecrated species can be thought of as changed by way of extrinsic reference only.

In fact, however, the case has been made by Catholic theologians that the profound ontological change required by Catholic faith consists precisely in the new transcendental reference of the species. To say that because the change has already occurred the food and drink have a new end or significance is temporarily comforting. The question is, has anything really been said? Rather, has not as much been said by the affirmation that neither bread nor wine is what it was because the prayer of the Church has changed it purpose, its signification, utterly? There is nothing about the change that sense can know. What is on the altar is now Christ's body and blood. It is such really sacramentally, not naturally or physically. That is to say, His real physical body is signified by this symbol which makes Him present.

The question of the new eucharistic theologians is, can not the total ontological or intrinsic change demanded by Catholic faith be accomplished by putting the admittedly unchanged species in a totally new relation to the heavenly body of Christ? That at least this much happens is certain in Catholic faith. The problem is, will it not suffice as the reality of the *transubstantiatio* of defined Catholic faith, and even express the mystery better? It may sound as if in such a theory "the bread and wine remain." By no means. Their appearances "remain." What is there, in virtue of sign, is another reality: Jesus Christ.

It hardly seems fair for those who have a philosophical theory on substance which covers the data to their satisfaction ("the substance of His body is present") to claim the stronger or the purer faith. Catholic faith, after all, is: "Jesus Christ is where formerly there had been bread and wine. The change is total: *transubstantiatio* describes it fittingly enough." It is not faith but philosophy, or the manipulation of words, which is often praised in place of faith.

Some unguarded things have evidently been written and said in the last few years in popular sources. Such is the testimony of the Pope. Schillebeeckx bears him out, quoting, however, only one phrase of Smits which was rectified between its periodical and book forms. The impression was given through the use of analogies, it seems, that the eucharistic meal was like any meal in which a host became better known to his guests in the sign of the food he lovingly prepared. The analogy is extraordinarily weak for the Eucharist unless it stresses the presence unique in all human experience of Christ, the host at the meal, in this sign.

Once these comparisons of doubtful worth are eliminated, however, a root difficulty remains. Our Lord is present in the Eucharist as offered to us. He is not present as accepted by us until, moved by the sign, we take in His person in faith. Any theology of Christ's real presence which considers His presence as offered, as *there,* as if this were the final matter is bound to to be puzzling to any Catholic who rightly asks: "And then?"

The Catholic faithful (this includes the clergy, of course) can be scandalized by any intimation from pulpit or press that Jesus Christ is not present, and present as adorable, under the eucharistic species. If there be any such intimation it is a danger to faith and must cease. Once the danger has been removed, the education of the faithful on the meaning of His eucharistic presence can begin. The Pope feared that the faith of many in the best-known eucharistic presence of Christ was being imperiled, and he took measures to protect their faith in this mystery. He left to others the important task of conveying the mystery in its fullness as the *Constitution on the Sacred Liturgy* brings it to us.

19.

THE MEANING OF ISRAEL
AS IDEA AND REALITY*

THERE IS A passage at the close of Shakespeare's *The Taming of the Shrew* in which Kate speaks in praise of woman's master, her spouse.

> Thy husband is thy lord, thy life, thy keeper,
> Thy head, thy sovereign, one that cares for thee,
> And for thy maintenance commits his body
> To painful labour both by sea and land . . .

In return for this service he,

> craves no other tribute at thy hands
> But love, fair looks and true obedience.

Such was the love affair between the Lord, the great God of the heavens and the earth, and tiny Israel. Indeed, the Bible is filled with little else. Those sacred books tell us nothing, really, except the story of that high romance. Yahweh, God of Israel, is the suitor, the strong lover who will do almost anything to keep the affection of His errant bride. Too often Israel is, in Shakespeare's language, a "foul, contending rebel and graceless traitor to her loving Lord." She first serves Him, then betrays Him, then repents, only to serve and fall again. Like any

* First published in *Torah and Gospel: Jewish and Catholic Theology in Dialogue*, Philip Scharper, ed., New York, 1966, pp. 215–228.

husband wronged, Yahweh grows furious: "Therefore, O harlot, hear the word of the Lord. Thus says the Lord God: Because . . . your shame has been discovered through your adulteries with your lovers . . . behold I will gather together all your lovers with whom you have taken pleasure and all whom you have loved, with all whom you have hated, and I will gather them together against you on every side, and will uncover your shame in their sight, and they shall see all your nakedness. And I will judge you as adulteresses and they that shed blood are judged, and bring upon you the blood of wrath and jealousy." (Ez. 16, 35–38)

Yahweh, God of love and mercy, of course did no such thing. Indeed, He hadn't the heart to do it. Being a God of love and mercy He promised her reconciliation, a thing unheard of, since it was strictly forbidden by the Law of Moses to take back one's wife after divorce. Yet, through the prophet Jeremiah the Lord says, "Return, O virgin Israel, return to these your cities. How long will you continue to stray, O rebellious daughter? For the Lord has created a new thing upon the earth: the woman returns to her husband [or: must encompass the man]." Jer. 31, 22)

I begin my presentation—there is no other place to begin— with the holy books which give testimony to the life of a people. These books are not themselves that history, that life, but they testify to it. And their testimony is true.

The two cities where the sacred writings of ancient Israel are held in honor are Judaism and Christianity. The two peoples agree on this: that there should not be two cities of God in the midst of men but one. The Jew says it is God's will that all the nations of the earth shall drink at the spring of holy wisdom which lies at the heart of his city. The Christian says that in company with Israel the nations have already been let drink of waters purer than mortal man can dream, not as suppliants or petitioners but as equals and brothers, as dwellers in the city with

208

full rights of citizenship, though not born there. Both Jew and Christian say what they say in faith. They would not dare to speak otherwise.

Meanwhile, the sacred books are the meeting ground where Jew and Christian can consort briefly as one, not two; briefly, because duality always lurks close by. The sacred writings lead to this great matter somehow, if not fully realized, says the Christian. The writings point to that same matter unfulfilled, the Jew must say. And we are two again. But briefly we were one, perhaps to be inseparably one again and forever through these holy books whose author is that God who is the Lord. The Jewish Scriptures in any case represent a hope, and specifically a hope for the religious unity of men.

More than all else, the sacred books are the bridge between brothers who are separated, for their words express the aspirations and the ideals of sons of a common Father. The Spirit of the Lord speaks to our spirit in these writings. Let pass what may, they will remain. They cannot change or lose what force they ever had. They can only be fulfilled in a greater divine event, yielding meanings they always possessed but meanings which men will come to know only slowly and painfully as the years unfold.

Many books written in our time seek to remind us of *the* Book. Some are written by Christians who assume that the Israelite experience is true, that the Christian experience is true, and that these experiences are not two but one. On this assumption they are one not as the two sides of a single coin are one, nor as a child is something of its mother and in that sense one with her, but as nothing else in all nature is one, though two.

I can write here neither as a learner from divine Wisdom who has become more learned, nor as an adolescent grown adult, without immediately offending Jew and Christian alike. How shall I express in human language the reality I seek to express when there is a mystery—a divine mystery—surrounding the people of Israel? With respect to this mystery perhaps the least apprehended truth is the basic Jewishness of Christianity, the latent Christianity of Judaism, and the near impossibility of speaking of the two in terms of a relation. When there is a condition of identity the word "relation" has no place. When one regards two things in relation he thereby assumes them to be distinct, disparate. How useless is our ordinary vocabulary in speaking of this wonder! The very fact that the situation is in some sense inexpressible leads us to realize that we are in the presence of authentic divine mystery.

The Hebrew scriptures, we remarked at the outset, tell the story of a great love. One thinks of how exasperating it must be for the Jew to hear that God sent love into the world with His Son, Jesus, and that before Jesus' time there was only covenant, justice, and law. And what of the basically unchristian ring to the phrase, "Christian charity," as if Christians were saying that Jesus is "the man who invented *ḥesed*"? Only if there has first been faith in a divine dispensation through Moses that is all *ḥesed we emeth*—"love and fidelity, grace and truth"—is it possible to speak of the Word become man as the fullness of grace and truth.

For the Christian the scriptures of Israel are a book of instruction and formation priceless in value—priceless for the Christian, we may say, in their "independent value" (if that phrase does not cut God off from His work). They are a compendium of prayer, they are the inexhaustible food of contemplation. These books are the well of Jacob to which parched and sinful humanity comes to draw water. The God of Jacob is there waiting to speak to that sinner, waiting to proffer the waters of eternal life.

For the ancient Jew the world's history was all but synonymous with Israel's history. If there was a significant difference between the two the Jew of old did not know it. Adam's sin meant the beginning of sin for all mankind. The relationship

210

between God and man consequent on that sin became the accepted condition of men on the earth, even as friendship with God had characterized man's primitive state. "The earth was corrupt in the sight of God, and it was filled with violence." (Gen. 6, 11)

But there was Noah, who was blameless. He rode out the storm in trust, and afterwards he knew how to offer holocausts which pleaded with their sweet odor. "When the bow is in the clouds I will look upon it . . . and remember the perpetual covenant between God and every living creature of flesh." (9, 14f.) Nor was God's fidelity fruitless, for a spared humanity meant heirs to the promise: Abram, son of Terah, received the call in the flourishing metropolis of Ur. "I will make a great nation of you. I will bless you and make your name great." (12, 2)

Thus does the strong alliance, the solemn covenant of friendship, tentatively begin. Later Abraham was to say to the Lord, "I am but dust and ashes." (18, 27) But he said it bravely and even ventured to ask, "What if ten [just] be found there?" "I will not destroy it [the city] for the sake of ten," said the Lord. (18, 32) And God promised him—the God who is faithful to His promise, "In your desendants all the nations of the earth shall be blessed, because you have obeyed me." (22, 18)

Since God is true to His word, the happiness of all men is to be found through this people made up of the descendants of Abraham according to the flesh. The nations will praise and love Him because of this people and its relation to Him. And if the promise means anything it means that this relationship is eternal. In the people Israel, in Abraham's seed, "The earth shall be filled with the knowledge of the glory of the Lord, as the waters cover the depths of the sea." (Heb. 2, 14) The heathen make song and saga but the prophets of Israel's God speak truth. They report His activity in their midst; they record the history of God with men. Through His promises to Abraham, Isaac, and

Jacob and their descendants His name is declared holy. A torrent of grace is poured out from age to age, and the sacred books record the flow.

But there must be some means for the two to communicate. In a matter so important there cannot be guesswork. If God is a living God and man a living soul, then surely there will be some way to converse. For His purpose, God uses the words of His prophets. When there is doubt that the words are really His, they are to be believed if there is a sign. Truly He is a hidden God (cf. Is. 45, 15) who must always act behind some veil of sense. Were it otherwise He would not be God but a man. God spoke His word on Sinai and upheld it with a sign. "The glory of the Lord settled upon Mount Sinai. The cloud covered it for six days, and on the seventh day he called Moses from the midst of the cloud. To the Israelites the glory of the Lord was seen as a consuming fire on the mountaintop." (Ex. 24, 16f)

This was the way of God with His people: always to communicate through holy ones and in circumstances that reminded His people that He alone is the Holy. "Indeed the Lord God does nothing without revealing his plan to his servants, the prophets." (Amos 3, 7) He is not the God of the philosophers and the sages, available to the subtle inquiries of their minds. No, God is the worker of marvelous works whose deeds and words are unmistakable. After them there can only come faith or unbelief. " 'Learn then that I, I alone, am God, and there is no god besides me'." (Dt. 32, 39) All other worship is idolatry. " 'Now, therefore, put away the strange gods that are among you and turn your hearts to the Lord, the God of Israel'." (Jos. 24, 23)

From Adam's day all Israel knew the lie that said, "Your eyes will be opened and you will be like God." (Gen. 3, 5) It was a base lie because no creature is like Him. Only for Him is it worth leaving country, kinsfolk, and a father's house. "To whom

can you liken me as an equal? says the Holy One" (Is. 40, 25),
for "I am the first, and I am the last; there is no God but me.
Who is like me? Let him stand up and speak, make it evident,
and confront me with it." (44, 6)

This jealous God does not see Israel give His glory to another
with equanimity but with wrath. If there is rumor of a town or
place in conquered lands that will not have Him for its only
God, the inhabitants must be tracked down and put to the sword.
All His works are right and all His ways are just, and He is able
to humble those who walk in pride.

God's name is Holy; He is the Lord. "This is my name forever;
this is my title for all generations." (Ex. 3, 15) From on high
He looks down on the sons of men and, knowing their sinfulness, demands of them the sacrifice—the gift—of an obedient
will. He commands that honor be given to father and mother.
He requires truthfulness, justice, brotherly love. Most of all, He
commands fidelity to Himself. A loving Father, He would have
offspring who are one seed. He is the shepherd of Israel and this
people is but one flock. "Have we not all one Father? Has not
the one God created us? Why then do we break faith with each
other, violating the covenant of our fathers? . . . For Judah has
profaned the temple which the Lord loves, and has married an
idolatrous woman." (Mal. 2, 10f.)

The Israelite had a concern for the past but he did not look
exclusively to the past. His was a religion primarily of hope in
events to come. He could endure life in virtue of a deliverance
that was sure to happen in the future. The night of the Passover
with its remembrance of liberation from Egypt, in a series of
events long behind the pious Jew, was but the token of a full
and future liberation. "Tomorrow shall the iniquity of the earth
be abolished and the Savior of the world—Yahweh—shall
reign over us.

In his work, *Homo Viator,* Gabriel Marcel speaks of hope as
establishing a relationship between the soul and time. Hope

213

always establishes an extremely logical connection between a return to the past (*nostos*) and something completely new (*kainon ti*). The aspiration can be expressed in the simple and seemingly contradictory words, "as before, but differently and better than before." Liberation, for the Jew and the Christian, is never a simple return to the *status quo;* it is that and much more, and even the contrary of that: an undreamed-of promotion, a transfiguration.

In what sense is it true that the kingdom of God is close at hand, that "the glory of the Lord shall be revealed, and all flesh shall see the salvation of our God" (Is. 40, 5)?

What is the reality described when we speak of "the deliverance from the perils that threaten us by reason of our sins?" (Collect, IV Sunday of Advent). How will the Lord Himself be stationed at the rampart of the city wall of Zion, the mountains, hills, and every woodland tree paying Him tribute by singing a song of praise? Even a little serious reflection by the believer, Jew or Christian, yields an answer to these questions.

He will come. Surely He will come and save. But in between there is the uncertainty, the longing. "Is it your coming that was foretold, or look we for another?" (Magnificat Antiphon, Second Sunday of Advent) They put the question to Jesus, but it is one that would have been put to many in that age of anguished expectation.

. . . say to those whose hearts are frightened: Be strong, fear not! Here is your God, he comes with vindication: with divine recompense he comes to save you. Then will the eyes of the blind be opened, the ears of the deaf be cleared; then will the lame man leap like a stag, then the tongue of the dumb will sing. Streams will burst forth in the desert, and rivers in the steppe. . . . A highway will be there, called the holy way; no one unclean may pass over it, nor fools go astray on it. No lion will be there, nor beast of prey go up to be met upon it. It is for those with a journey to make, and on it the redeemed will walk. Those whom the Lord has ransomed will return and enter Zion singing, crowned with everlasting joy; they will meet with joy and gladness, sorrow and mourning will flee.—(Is. 35, 4–10)

There was not much more, really, that a poet of Israel could say about the days of deliverance. How could he praise the God of his fathers better than to say that in the days of Messiah the dispersed captives would throng the city of Jerusalem once more and fill the air with their pious shouts? The Lord Himself would come and save. In that day all the woes that plagued a mystified Near East would be no more: the withered limbs, the deafness, the eyes sightless from birth, the all-pervading thirst. Surely the Lord would destroy them all in the last days. How could He show Himself the vindicator of His people—their *go'el*, their ransomer or bail bondsman who was one of their blood—if He did not wipe the tear from every eye, if His people could not "draw water with joy from the springs of salvation" (Is. 12, 3), pure water flowing from the temple, "for the cleansing of sin and uncleanness" (Zech. 13, 1)?

Israel's prophets used to dream about what the messianic age would be like. The Spirit of the Lord would pour out streams of water on the dry earth; the new Israel in that day would be a spring "whose waters never fail" (Is. 58, 11). Like the four rivers of Eden, like the sweet waters of Mara near the springs of Elim, a garden fountain from Lebanon would make the desert bloom in that age; the lame would walk and the halt would cavort with joy. Indeed, all this was fitting since the Lord Himself would come on a straight path and a high road.

It was not a fiction, as we know, not a flight of Oriental fancy. For when He came in the person of Jesus, as the Christian holds—Lord and Messiah in one, surely not Yahweh's only coming in the flesh or His last—He came on the filled valleys, the hills made low, the straightened ways of a few hearts prepared. He came to Zion, the holy mountain, and He spoke to the men of Israel, in their city and their temple, of the signs that meant fulfillment. And some believed that Jesus came from God and some did not. Later, Gamaliel put the meaning of Jesus to a pragmatic test. "For if this plan or work is of men it will be overthrown; but if it is of God, you will not be able to overthrow it. Else perhaps you might find yourselves fighting even against God." (Acts 5, 38f.)

Why does God speak? Why does the one God give utterance? Surely to hear a response, in love, from His own people—from his creature Adam, man whom He sent in love to rule the earth through serving Him alone.

But Adam is no longer one as God made Him in love. Like a potter's vessel he has fallen to the earth and has shattered into a thousand pieces. A thousand? Yes, but chiefly into two pieces. He is an elder brother and a younger, a son long faithful and a brash young wastrel. Adam is Sem and he is Chanaan; he is Isaac and he is Ishmael; he is Jacob and he is Esau; he is Juda and his brothers and he is the Gentile; he is the Jew and he is the Christian; he is two who are not one, except to their Father for whom they will ever be one as He is one.

Speaking from the side of the Christian brother, we have not had enough trust in our Father to believe that. In proposing the test of Gamaliel, we have proposed that it be put only in one way, or in such a way as to achieve but a single result. We Christians have told the Jews what they ought to be, religiously, and have not bothered to learn that they do not remotely fit our specifications. We have said, "You ought not to be Jews at all; but since you are you had better be Orthodox. That's the good kind." But when Jews became Conservative and Reformed and when some of them began to eat pork and everything else (saying that in those matters the scriptures are not to be interpreted literally), we said they had lost all faith. What we forgot was that we, centuries earlier, had declared our own freedom from those prescriptions of the Law and any such view of the scriptures. We Christians assumed that our sacred scriptures continued to be theirs, ignoring the fact that the equality of the traditions of the ancients with the books of the bible had been claimed as far back as Jesus' day. Our learned Christian men quote Isaiah and Jeremiah for the instruction of the Jews (a trap I have here not escaped), while their sages are frequently concerned with Talmudic lore, something we Christians have not bothered to master.

We declared Judaism static, lifeless, a vestigial thing which exists not by divine right but if anything by a terrifying act of disobedience. Yet Judaism, seemingly unconscious of the ban, has developed and found new expression continuously. All this while we ourselves have been doing a perilous thing, though we say that the Spirit of God keeps us from doing ultimate harm to our faith: as a people we have forgotten our roots, we have neglected our scriptures. Oh, we Christians can still name the great patriarchs and prophets and recite their lives in outline, but we tend to make one great leap from Adam to Christ. Of the Lord Jesus and Mary His mother we still affirm proudly that they were Jews. However, what all of this should mean to us we Christians have largely forgotten. The Jewish antecedents of our faith remain a fact, but a fact without much meaning to us. Yet we may not forget that what we call the New Law—another perilous term, for it has about it the ring of God's unfaithfulness to His promise—was impossible without the Old; that religion meant to Jesus what it meant to Abraham, Moses, David, the prophets. Each of the two religious cultures, Judaism and Christianity, has gone its own path of development, with the result that the fact of common ancestry according to the Spirit seems far-off and in a sense unimportant.

May I propose a way back, at least from the Christian side, to the ramparts leading to that bridge-to-the-Father which for us is Christ? It may seem so trivial as scarcely to deserve attention.

You remember, perhaps, what the elders of the Jews said

217

when they went to Jesus and urged Him strongly to heal the centurion's slave? "He deserves to have you do this for him, for he loves our nation, and it was he who built us our synagogue." (Lk. 7, 5) In other words, he loves our people. Now make what you will of that, they said to Jesus.

How we Christians come to love Jews as people is of no special consequence, but *that* we love them—this is imperative. We may see in them signs of a divine mystery, "the one indisputable proof of the existence of God," as Barth says. We need not be so metaphysical or so ultimate about it, however. To see in the Jew our estranged brother whom we are called to love above all men and, much more importantly, to like, this is enough. In any case, if we Christians fail we may be sure that we have earned our Father's wrath.

If the Catholic is thoroughly filled with the bible and his own liturgy—those two undying monuments of Hebrew thought—he has made the best remote preparation possible to embrace the Jew as a brother. He has done very little by way of immediate preparation, however, because, if for no other reason, most Jews do not know their Scriptures any better than do Catholics. Such Jews can be no more offended by the claims of an incarnation or by Paul's teaching on conditional reprobation than if a Hottentot were to press these claims. In the main, these people know that they are Jews and that there is a kind of natural protection afforded them if they remain Jews. They are afraid to step out of the circle and lose all.

This leads to some perhaps unattractive conclusions for the Catholic. He must learn Jewish Judaism, not Catholic Judaism; he must know something about a Simchas Torah, the ordinary Friday night service, the modern dietary observances; he must give outward signs—heartfelt signs—that Jewishness is a thoroughly acceptable human condition and that the Jewish religion is a way to serve God in reverence and love; he must even try

218

to comprehend the United Jewish Appeal and the case for the State of Israel.

This process of understanding is a conversion of the self, and all conversion is painful. It ceases to be a question, as it now is, of how much the Jew will have to change to be one with the Catholic if the Catholic has first changed to become one with him. For as Paul wrote long ago (Eph. 2, 14), Christ has broken down the wall that was there between Catholic and Jew. While that may be true in some radical cosmic sense, it is not true in fact. Christians have seen to that by their lack of faith in what God has accomplished in Jesus, though they manage to keep talking about it.

I conclude by holding out the hope that Catholic education—not necessarily Catholic school education only—is currently in a tentative state of reform. The stirrings of Vatican II, so often unsatisfactory even to us Catholics, are those of a giant waking from sleep. He has almost forgotten how to walk. He is capable of being a bully, like all giants, and one is right to fear him. But if he can learn to walk in gentleness and brotherhood and absolute trust in God, there is everything to hope for.

We must leave ourselves open to what of God is at work among us. What do you and I mean to the legions of black Africa, to teeming India, to China in the design of God? Surely they are His sons, too. And surely our behavior borders on the frivolous if we do not come to see who we are to each other and stop acting out that oldest of human archetypes: brothers who are so far separated because they are so close.

20.

THE AGE OF FIRST CONFESSION*

THE SYNDICATED CATHOLIC PRESS carried a wire story in early June of this year indicating that in the diocese of Richmond, Virginia, beginning next autumn, the sacrament of penance will normally be administered to children one year after they have made their first communion (presumably therefore at the age of eight), and that the age of confirmation is to rise from around the age of eleven to around the age of thirteen. One recalls immediately the directives deferring the first reception of penance issued by Petrus Moors, the late bishop of Roermond, Holland, on May 15, 1964, which proposed the start of an instruction period on the virtue and sacrament of penance in the third grade, communal sacramental celebrations of this virtue in fourth grade, and individual reception of absolution by children in the fifth grade. First communion is normally to be distributed in the second grade. (Cf. *The Living Light*, 2, 1 [Spring, 1965], 146–55 for the documentation.)

There probably have been other instances in the U.S. of attempts at diocesan-wide settlement of some of the pastoral problems attending the first reception of the sacrament of penance, but if so the present writer has missed them. The change reported above, consisting not only in the separation of the two sacraments but their reversed order, comes in response

* From the Proceedings of the CTSA, June 21, 1967.

to a widespread demand of pastoral theologians.[1] This demand is twofold: that the first reception of the bread of life should not be clouded over by an introspective search for guilt in childhood, thus marring it forever after by close association with this guilt search (the danger of the child's supposing that the Eucharist must always be preceded by penance is one that is largely past, I should think); and the demand that pastoral practice concerning penance—virtue and sacrament—should not get off to a bad start by the sacrament's being administered on the wide scale to those who are not fit subjects for it; some would even go so far as to say, "valid subjects for it." The Richmond proposal attends to the first problem, namely that of association; aside from allowing for another twelve months in the maturing process it does not seriously attend to the second problem, namely that of the capability of eight-year-olds to profit from this experience, whether as fit subjects for forgiveness or as optimum learners at this age about the reality of personal sin—strictly so-called—later in life.[2]

[1] Those who favor a change in the discipline would include Ludwig Bertsch, S.J., "Der Rechte Zeitpunkt der Erstbeicht," *Stimmen der Zeit,* 175 (1965), pp. 225–62; Josef Dreissen, "Die jüngste Entwicklung der Erstbeicht und Erstkommunion im Bistum Roermond," *Katechetische Blätter,* 89 (1964), p. 498, n. 6; J. van Haaren, "De eerste biecht," *De Bazuin,* 43 (1962–63), n. 33; J. A. Jungmann, *Handing on the Faith,* New York, 1959, p. 303; J. Hofinger, "The Age Most Appropriate for First Confession," *Good Tidings,* 5 (1966), pp. 5–10; Eve Lewis, "Children and the Sacrament of Penance," *The Month,* 220 (1965), pp. 28–36. Opposed are G. Lobo, S.J., "Children's Confessions," *Clergy Monthly,* 31 (1967), pp. 94–101; M. Huftier, "De la confession des enfants," *L'Ami du Clergé,* 75 (1965), pp. 332–34; Pierre Ranwez, S.J., "The Sacraments of Initiation and the Age for First Confession," *Lumen Vitae,* 20 (1965), pp. 9–24.

[2] The Words of Aquinas on the subject are helpful here. He writes: Cum vero usum rationis habere inceperit, non omnino excusatur a culpa venialis et mortalis peccati. Sed primum quod tunc homini cogitandum occurrit, est deliberare de seipso. Et si quidem seipsum ordinaverit ad debitum finem, per gratiam consequetur remissionem originalis peccati. Si vero non ordinet seipsum ad debitum finem, secundum quod in illa aetate est capax discretionis, peccabit mortalitas, non faciens quod in se

221

From the fact that infants have traditionally been baptized absolutely and that the unconscious have been both absolved and anointed conditionally, it is no doubt possible to put forward a sacramental theology which will justify a rite which speaks of absolving from personal sin those who at the time of reception are incapable of personal sin. They are, after all, members of a sinful race and belong to a Church of sinners despite their baptismal justification, hence they can be considered fit subjects for a rite concerned with removing the guilt of the post-baptismal sin which they will almost certainly incur. I simply spell out the main line of argument that could be developed in terms of human and ecclesial solidarity in sin, and the possibility of subsequent, fully conscious ratification of a sign participated in as a child.

Since, however, penance traditionally befits those Christians who have, in fact, sinned seriously after baptism, the doctrinal and pastoral theological justification for administering it to the young has been that they are capable of serious sin after the age of "reason" or "discretion." Even if this may not be true, it is fallen back on as axiomatic that they are capable of venial sin (the very matter put in question by Aquinas). Ranwez sees in the confessions of the young a ratification of their baptism as infants, in an attempt to keep the triad of initiation baptism, confirmation, and Eucharist somehow together.[3]

It has almost been a watchword of Catholic orthodoxy to hold that somewhere around seven years of age a child is capable of

---

est. Et ex tunc non erit in eo peccatum veniale sive mortali, nisi postquam totum fuerit sibi per gratiam remissum. (Ia IIae, q. 89, a. 6c)

Exactly when a person "orders himself to his proper end"—God as *bonum salutare*—is the very matter in question. Joseph J. Sikora, writing on "Faith and First Moral Choice," in *Sciences Ecclésiastiques,* 17 (1965), 327–37, favors the possibility of a "formal and actual, although preconscious," knowledge of God as one's end; in this case, "the truth of the doctrine of St. Thomas that this first moral act must result in either mortal sin or justification seems clear," p. 337.

[3] Ranwez, *op. cit.,* pp. 10–13.

committing serious sin. If the case should be—on theological, not on psychological grounds—that the first moral choice which properly deserves that name is an option which can justify in faith and charity, and conversely can reprobate in virtue of the preference of self or creatures to God, then the popular pastoral position which holds that seven-year-olds are capable of venial sin at least, in virtue of analogous moral decisions whereby theirs is real but analogous moral conduct, must also be abandoned.[4] I repeat, if such a theory is correct, then a child or adolescent becomes capable of committing any and all sin, grave or light, at the same time. In the twofold event that the making of this fundamental option for or against God comprises the first possibility of venial sin as well as mortal, and that the possibility of making it does not occur until high adolescence, we then have a whole Church-full of little people regularly submitting deviant childhood behavior to adjudication which cannot be termed sinful even by analogy, our usual description of the character of venial offense.

We are not even right in saying that these actions (childhood lies, disobedience, anger, sexual curiosity) are fittingly confessed because they are the raw material for post-adolescent sinfulness. Their very material coincidence with sinful behavior without the essential character of sin, which is a fundamental choice against God and his love, seems to disqualify them from being submitted for absolution lest the confusion between normal childhood development and genuine moral fault be implanted for life. Yet to argue in this way is to get ahead of ourselves, for the question at issue is whether the young—say children of six through ten, twelve, or fourteen—find themselves in a situation in response to which the sacrament of penance is fitting behavior

[4] F. J. Connell, cited below, n. 7, seems to hold this position, p. 269. So do John J. Lynch, S.J., "Notes on Moral Theology," *Theological Studies,* 26 (1965), pp. 277, 657f., and G. Lobo, S.J., *op. cit.,* pp. 97f.

on the part of the whole Church. Theirs is a "condition of sin," they have a dawning moral consciousness, and at this age they need a fitting pedagogy of the virtue of penance—of which the sacramental discipline is but a part. Question: Is the sacrament of penance the right expression of the virtue and discipline of penance at this point in childhood? Everything hangs on the meaning of the phrases *"usum rationis"* and *"aetas discretionis"* and this paper will attempt to explore their meaning.

Needless to say, human development is a continuum. Since this is so it is not to be supposed that even the most dependable research into child psychology will yield a certain year when all of youth has arrived at the moral consciousness proper to responsible human beings. The best that can be hoped for is "around seven," "around ten," "around fourteen." No one supposes that every blunder in pastoral psychology can be avoided but only the more serious ones, and with the greatest number. The hope is that in adolescent and adult life the saving sign of reconciliation which penance is will be resorted to lovingly, at need, by Roman Catholics. They will have begun to seek it out from the time they first enjoyed the *usum rationis,* whenever that may be.

The Code of Canon Law requires the annual reception of the Eucharist and the annual reception of penance at the same time, namely when a person has come to "the age of discretion, that is, the use of reason."[5] This age is not specified at that point in the Code, but elsewhere it is stated that all who have attained the use of reason except those who are not yet seven are bound to observe the ecclesiastical law unless a law itself expressly states the contrary.[6] There is a diminished discipline with respect

[5] Can. 859, §1 (Eucharist); 906 (penance—same phrase used). The presumption is that the precept of annual penance binds those who have serious sins to confess ("omnia peccata sua").

[6] Cf. Can. 12; 88, §3.

to penal legislation.[7] In Canon 88, §3, it is defined that those who have attained their seventh year are presumed to have reached the age of reason. I think there can be no doubt that Canon Law takes for granted that seven-year-olds are capable of mortal sin and hence need to go to confession.[8]

In this legal corpus the child is considered a *homunculus* or small adult. Throughout the more than fifteen centuries of normative sway of the concepts basic to the Code, the idea of developmental psychology was known in only the crudest way. The rhetorical question which appears regularly in modern pastoral theological writing, "Would any court think of condemning a child of ten or twelve to death for a crime?" rings hollow in light of the fact that as late as the eighteenth century in England they were still hanging children for petty theft. There is even record of the hangman's having to pull the child's tiny body by the feet since its weight alone would not suffice. If the assumptions of Church law concerning child development are gravely wrong, as some contend they are, there should be no difficulty in revising the canons these assumptions led to, in light of better contemporary knowledge. It is sufficiently widely held that all legal and disciplinary settlements in Church life are products of their times; certain Council documents like that on the Church in the modern world make this very clear. Hence there should be no basic difficulty in revising the law.

[7] The canons on the age proper to the incurring of ecclesiastical penalties for crimes speak of the diminution of guilt as one descends from puberty to pre-puberty to infancy. Cf. Cans. 2204, 2230.

[8] Robert O'Neil and Michael Donovan in *Psychological Development and the Concept of Mortal Sin,* Chicago, 1966, go into the history of this canonical presumption in some detail. "The use of the arbitrary age of seven years to mark the beginning of the power of rational evaluation of motives and goals . . . derives from the jurisprudential norms embodied in the ancient *Corpus Iuris Civilis* of the Byzantine Emperor Justinian I, promulgated in 529 A.D. This norm of Roman civil law was incorporated into the general law of the Church," p. 12. This pamphlet of 33 pages is based on material which first appeared in *Insight, A Review of Religion and Mental Health.*

A graver difficulty for some than the Code is the fact that Pope Pius X in his decree *Quam singulari* on children's communions puts the use of reason at "about the seventh year" and adds that "from that time on the obligation begins of fulfilling both precepts, confession and communion."[9] Some theologians see in both the Code and the papal decree, but more especially the latter, what they call "the ruling of the Church" or "the attitude of the Church," hence a position which one challenges only in a spirit of offense against Catholic faith in the papal office.[10]

Quam singulari does hold, however, that

> The obligation of confession and communion binding the child rests principally on those who must care for the child, that is the parents, the confessor, the teachers, and the parish priest. . . . The custom of not admitting children to confession when they have reached the use of reason or of never absolving them is to be reprobated thoroughly (*omnino reprobanda*).[11]

F. J. Connell derives from the first statement the warning that no pastor may withhold penance from a child whose parents insist that it precede communion. Quite clearly the target of the pope's stricture in the second statement is the lazy pastor who does not wish to give any time to children's needs. It should be obvious that the primacy of parents over clergy and teachers is intended by the order in which those persons who are presumed to know the child's deepest thoughts are listed: parents, confessor, teachers, parish priest. It is interesting to observe that the child's own demand for first confession is not made much of by theologians who write in favor of his ability to sin grievously. The conduct of adults is the chief matter

---

[9] *DS* 2137 [3530].

[10] Cf. Francis J. Connell, C.SS.R., "Answers to Questions," *The American Ecclesiastical Review*, 151 (1964), 268.

[11] *DS* 2140 [3533]; 2143 [3535].

discussed, and yet it is the child who theoretically should be most conscious of his grave spiritual need.

The case can be made, I think, that *Quam singulari* as it is worded requires no special Church-wide or diocesan-wide legislation to authorize today's pastors—understood to mean bishops —to instruct their adult parishioners and their children in such a way that the sacrament will not be asked for until the "use of reason," meaning as advanced an age—derived from the serious study of pastoral theology—as the bishop may propose to parents and children. In such case he would have to be careful to indicate why the centuries-old norm used by Church law and Pope Pius X is still "on the books," so to say. He must have an equal care for the consciences of both the traditionalists among his parishioners who know how the law reads and those who are shocked by the retention of such a norm when the delicate psyches of children are at stake.

Connell says he does not believe it can be proved psychologically that children are *always* (italics his) to be excused from the possibility of grave sin for the several years following their seventh year, though they may be *sometimes*.[12] He concludes: "I do not think that the procedure of Holy Communion before confession has sufficient arguments in its favor to warrant a change in our traditional custom."[13] Presumably, from this statement, if it were "proved psychologically" and if the arguments in favor of the change were sufficient he would require that "our traditional custom" yield. In that case the principle *contra factum non est argumentum* would guide him. The "fact" he asks for, however, is the psychological proof that no seven-year-old can sin mortally. This proof, we suggest, is not forthcoming since the science of psychology does not provide "proofs" about cognitive or evaluative judgments. What it does supply is indications about human behavior in childhood on the

12 Connell, *op. cit.*, p. 268.
13 *Ibid.*, p. 269.

basis of which improved pastoral practice can be begun. Since current pastoral practice is based on similar indications and not on "proof" there should be no difficulty here.

Some pastors find it sobering to consider the possibility that small children may be living in a state of unforgiven mortal sin. They are likewise worried about their being launched early on a "habit of sin." Still, one cannot escape the conclusion that the scruples of moral theologians derive from sources other than sustained worry about youthful enemies of God abroad in the world. These, we suggest, are mainly four: (1) the observation, from the limited experience of such theologians of the young (much of it in the confessional), that small children can be intelligent, willful, and capable of verbalizing their guilt, hence—in the theologians' reckoning—*capaces peccati mortalis;* (2) the recollection of the theologians' own remembered intelligence and tender conscience at an early age (this, we tentatively suggest, may be the most influential factor of all); (3) the fear that no "school" of pastoral preparation exists to prepare the young for sorrow for sin as adults if the sacrament of penance is not used early in this role, coupled with the suspicion that confessions of devotion are being impugned as part of the stress on the incapacity of children to commit mortal sin; (4) the fear that the Church will "lose face" if, in its official teaching, it has long been wrong over a matter so important as "the age of reason" and the proffering of this sacrament to subjects incapable of its chief benefit, or, as some would say, of any benefit. This last consideration touches immediately on the theme of this convention: can the science of theology, pastoral in this case, come to conclusions at variance with the Church's teaching authority in such a way as to provide a corrective for the exercise of that authority?

In proceeding to a tentative solution of some of the problems which attend the age of first confession, we should keep in mind that there is question here of part of the discipline of a sacrament which has had a very checkered history in both East and West. Never did the Church presume to say who could and could not commit serious sin, who had and had not committed it. The most that was ever spelled out was the overt behavior which deserved public censure. It is a confusion for either side in this dispute to claim that knowledge of either the possibility or the fact of sin by Christians of any age is the point at issue. What the Church has done is demanded *metánoia* or conversion to the Lord in all its members. The Church has instructed its members to search their hearts and make confession—sometimes public, sometimes private—of their guilt. The Church has had various disciplines and catechetical practices with respect to the need for penance. One of these—the one best known to the West, beginning some time before the year 1000—has been the submission of the guilt one is conscious of to a priest in private for God's forgiveness through Christ and the Church. The point at issue is, does the practice of proposing to seven-year-olds that they receive this sacrament because they may very well need it (viz., to be rid of serious sin) accord well or ill with our knowledge of the mental and emotional condition of children at this age? In general, does this practice square with what can be deduced by adults of the realities of childhood?

A Church-wide law or Western Church-wide law is made for the general run of men. It does not try to deal with every exception: the precocious, the retarded, the juvenile saint or sinner. God can take care of the exceptions. Not everything needs to be done by the Church *ad cautelam*. The whole faith community *does* need to conduct itself in such a way that it will instruct the young well, relieve them of youthful anxieties and not multiply them, and give to the young the means to Christian holiness they need when it seems they need them.

One could, at this point, present the results of studies in the development of moral consciousness done over several decades by scholars such as Arnold Gesell and Frances Ilg,[14] Jean Piaget,[15] H. Werner,[16] and Leonard Kohlberg[17]; to them one could add the studies in the consciousness of guilt done by the Roman Catholics Eve Lewis,[18] Charles Sandron,[19] and J. J. Larivière.[20] The evidence is overwhelming that the thinking of the young is syncretic or global, that it is non-logical, concrete, and non-relational. As late as the age of eleven or twelve years, according to Piaget, concepts are not readily comprehended and two-way relationships are mastered only with difficulty. The higher level of thought, which is articulated, abstract, and relational, is placed by Werner at between thirteen and fifteen years of age. Kohlberg says that by the first grade most children know the basic taboos in our society, namely what things adults are against, although often they do not know why they are against them. He proposes three levels of awareness or response: The Pre-Moral Level (punishment and obedience; instrumental hedonism), The Morality of Conventional Role Conformity (approval of others; authority-maintaining morality), and the Morality of Self-Accepted Moral Principles. The last two of his six "types" are the morality of contract and democratically accepted law and the morality of individual principles and conscience. In his studies, chronological age correlates high with moral internalization whereas I.Q. correlates low with it, indicating that high intelligence alone cannot overcome the development obstacle. None of the authors cited above considers

[14] (In collaboration with Louise B. Ames and Glenna E. Bullis) *The Child from Five to Ten,* New York, 1946, esp. "The Ethical Sense," pp. 403–21.

[15] *The Moral Judgment of the Child,* New York, 1965.

[16] *Comparative Psychology of Mental Development,* New York, 1948.

[17] "Moral Development and Identification," *Sixty-Second Yearbook of the National Society for the Study of Education,* Chicago, 1963.

[18] *Op. cit.*

[19] "End Primary School Catechetical Knowledge," *Lumen Vitae,* XII, 2 (1957), pp. 291–300.

[20] *Connaissances catéchistiques et control objectif,* Quebec, 1961.

conceptual thinking possible in a consistent and sustained way before eleven to thirteen years of age. Most of them would put the perfection of moral awareness somewhere between thirteen and fifteen years.

These psychological data do not settle who is and who is not capable of mortal sin. They do establish that early childhood, up through and including age seven, has memory and mimicry as its faculties better developed than thought. This fact can easily deceive adults as to what children "know" about behavior. Children know what they remember having been told about behavior; they do not readily make it their own possession. Social acceptance is a high-value item with them; they regret or are sorry for what they know it behooves them to be sorry for. In general they are not yet capable even by age eleven of a genuine reciprocal relation with other human beings, much less with God; yet the latter relation is the essence of Christian virtue, as its absence is of sin. We are not maintaining that conceptual thought is the only avenue to a personal commitment in faith. There is such a thing as a preconceptual and prejudgmental reaching out to the good, that Good which saves. Evaluative cognition in its perfection—i.e., the type proper to adult ethical life—comes late in the lives of most young people, namely with the onset of puberty. This is not the same as to say that the first opportunity to accept grace consciously or refuse it comes at that time. When that is, no man knows or needs to know. What the Church must do is conduct itself in such a way that no false ideas about imputability and sin are wrongly deduced from its penitential practice. Moral awareness comes slowly and gradually. Something that seems to resemble it comes long before it, standing with respect to it in the relation of acorn to oak. The acorn may not be declared an oak by fiat; the properties of the tree may not be assigned to the fruit on the theory that they are there latently or in potency. They are not there, in fact, now, and the acorn that is dealt with as if it

231

were an oak can be crushed or stunted by any such anticipation of its possibilities. Similarly, the child who will as an adolescent or adult freely choose for or against God may not be assumed to be capable of such free choice at every moment of his development. He may come to be that adult provided he is not untimely assumed to be such beforehand.

The small child needs help in coming on to an awareness of his sinfulness and his need for repentance as he comes to realize his latent power to choose for and against God in his daily life. The whole Church must help him in this. Is not the sacrament of penance the best means to school him in the need for repentance? Some say that it is. Ranwez deplores the standard catechesis on this sacrament—admitting readily that it is full of bad theology, bad psychology, and bad liturgy. He asks that this catechesis be done well, and if it is he sees no cogent arguments against early confession. The child of six is in an optimum condition of openness, he holds, to the awakening of his religious sense. From the fact that he tends to think globally the child can take the whole rite of conscious initiation in as a unit: penance, confirmation, and Eucharist in that order. Ranwez admits that penance should probably be administered to some *with* confession between seven and eight and a half, and for others be a "first celebration on the subject of confession" (p. 25); in this way he attends to the problem of differences in maturation. Ranwez holds that if the child is not opened to his religious possibilities at six or seven there is real question whether this can successfully be done at nine or ten. For him, the one is a necessary preliminary to the other.

I concede readily with him that this is so. At the same time, while holding for a beginning of the catechesis on penance at the early age of six, I nonetheless do not think that administering the sacrament at seven is wise. I propose, rather, experimenting to discover whether ten or eleven should be the first time at which children confess individually, though they may have received absolution communally before that. My proposal, it should be needless to say, makes sense only in a context of a parish or school life where there is a good liturgical celebration of all the sacraments, chiefly the Eucharist and penance, and where the formal catechesis on penance has been carried on in well-planned stages culminating in the sacrament. My reason for the deferment—on those terms, understand—is that I am convinced that any earlier attempts to teach the meaning of mortal sin to the young will end in convicting them of mortal sin in a state of false conscience. No matter what delicacy is employed, very shortly the discussion will arrive at what is, or could be, mortal sin for them. Given their stage of psychological development and their studiousness to please, given their response to authority figures (sisters and clergy in particular, and all catechists and teachers in preference to all parents), children will accommodate themselves. They will *have* mortal sins.

In this sense I agree fully with the theologians who say that small children can sin seriously from a subjective point of view. They can because they have been taught to think they can, and since this is so they will not know well into adolescence or adult life whether they can or not. Genuine *metánoia* or *conversio* to God, the real purpose of confession, is so important that it should not be threatened by anything, least of all by a counterfeit of itself. The words used in expressing sorrow may be the same, the ideas discussed may be the same, but the reality is different. A real turning away from self and creatures to God has very probably not taken place. Worst of all, it is thought by both adults and children that it has, at least in some childlike or beginning way. The child was fed meat when it could only assimilate milk. If it would gag or choke before people's eyes they might then stop the feeding process. But the meat seems to go down and because it does all alike are deceived. The harm that was done is apparent only years later in psychiatrists' offices, in broken marriages which have sexual ignorance or false

233

guilt as their basis, in the broken lives of those who have been ordained as priests or professed as religious, in the continuing childishness of the confessions of adults and their corresponding inability to conceive genuine sorrow over real sins.

I should like to make it clear that I favor as the primary goal an improved catechesis for the young on sin and repentance. This will include good beginnings in these matters by parents, which in turn means good adult formation by clergy and other teachers. I include the deferment of the sacrament of penance as an important, even a necessary part of good catechesis. I do not think that the deferment of the sacrament should ever be thought of as an independent good. Such a procedure would undoubtedly induce fewer traumas, but if it came after a vacuum of catechesis on humanity-wide and personal sin and guilt, then indeed the question, "How could you ever get them to confess?" would be valid. Ten or eleven is not a good time to start from the egg something that is of great importance for life.

My compelling reason for omitting the confession of sins while pressing for an effective catechesis of penance is the evidence provided by those who know the consciences of the young best, both scientifically and non-scientifically. They have not "proved" that the young cannot commit serious sins, any more than the assumption and long-standing practice of the Church have "proved" that they can. What child experts have established is a set of clear indications pointing to the need of a pastoral practice which will omit trying to inform children on the nature of *hamartía*, the reality of sin, when they appear incapable of such assimilation. We are going to act on a probability in this matter in any case, and I suggest that the state of childhood incapacity is the greater probability. In the case of children who may be guilty of serious sin before God in childhood, they should be given enough help both in their penance catechesis to conceive, and in celebration to express, sufficient sorrow that their guilt will be wiped away. Banking on such extra-sacramental forgiveness does not derogate from the sacrament of penance. It is rather a vote of confidence of the whole Church with respect to what was once called *poenitentia secunda* and *baptismus laboriosus*.

Perhaps Paul Horgan says all that I have been trying to say in his childhood memoir *Things As They Are*,[21] which begins this way (the first chapter is entitled "Original Sin"):

"Richard, Richard," they said to me in my childhood, "when will you begin to see things as they are?"

But they forgot that children are artists who see and enact through simplicity what their elders have lost through experience. The loss of innocence is a lifelong process—the wages of original sin. Guilt is the first knowledge.

"Richard," they said, "are you terribly sorry?"

"Oh, yes."

[21] New York, 1964.